THIS IS THAT

Also by Anand Mehrotra

LIBERATION

An Interpretation of
Isha Upanishad

THIS IS THAT

Patanjali's Yoga Sutras

Padas 1 and 2

Anand Mehrotra

Sattva Publications

Cover photo from the collection of the

Sattva Yoga Academy

ISBN: 978-81-939882-1-3

Published by Sattva Publications
Rishikesh, India

This is That and That is This.

This is not somewhere else and

That is not somewhere else.

They are just different levels of here.

You are This and you are That

and everything else in between.

~ Anand

Dedicated to Maharaji

Stay Connected

Sattva Yoga
@sattvayogaacademy

Sattva Yoga Academy
@sattvayogaacademy

Sattva Yoga Academy
sattvayogaacademy.com

SATTVA
YOGA

Table of Contents

Anand Mehrotra

Born and raised in Rishikesh, Anand Mehrotra was mentored by his Guru from childhood leading him to deeper states of self-realization. As a young man, he travelled extensively throughout India studying the teachings from the Vedic and Tantric traditions. He developed Sattva Yoga as a method through which people of all backgrounds, cultures and experiences can discover and embrace their own true nature. It is a practice relevant for any time in which we live, a profound journey of personal evolution that guarantees one's transformation when one commits to it. Since then he has taught hundreds of students across the world including the USA, Australia, Europe and Russia, guiding them toward their own self-realization.

Along with founding Sattva Yoga, he has established the Sattva Yoga Academy, a leading yoga teacher training school in Rishikesh, Sattva Connect, online teachings and classes, and Sattva Retreat, a global destination. His visionary approach to yoga has led to the establishment of the Sattva Summit, a unique annual gathering that explores the nature of consciousness and celebrates the potential for humanity to live with a radical sense of aliveness, purpose and freedom. In addition to being a master teacher, Anand has also created the charitable initiatives: Khushi Foundation and Sattva Foundation.

Anand has been featured in many award-winning documentaries including *The Highest Pass*. He has led several impactful, and undoubtedly transformational, motorcycle journeys over the Himalayas. His teachings invite participants to break the limitations of their own mind and to experience themselves as fully present in their lives. He has dedicated his own life to honoring the knowledge and wisdom of the Himalayas, to protecting the integrity of the powerful techniques contained within the ancient practices and to guiding others to their own self-realization through yoga.

A Brief History of Yoga

In the beginning there is yoga. And in the end there is yoga. Because in yogic terms there is no time, so there is no beginning. Or middle. Or end. It's a great paradox. But in this realm and with this nervous system and understanding, linear time is how we perceive our world and so, in linear time, Shiva is considered by the yogis to be the first master of yoga. Shiva, also known as Mahakala, and his great consort, the goddess and Divine Mother, Kali, are the great destroyers of time. Therefore, the history of yoga fundamentally starts from a timeless domain. You may have to think about that for a moment, but it's very important for us to remember it, because when we speak about the history of yoga, it's only a history on one level, a linear history for the sake of intellectual understanding. For practitioners of yoga there is no history of yoga. There is only yoga.

It is also important for us to realize that, in the historical context, yoga was not considered something you did separately in life. Yoga was life. Yoga is life. All the ancient scriptures pertaining to yoga are really discussing life as a whole, yoga as a holistic practice. You see, there was no one central yoga authority figure, no controlling organization. This reductionist view we have now is a very modern phenomenon that has come about in the last five decades. So we are not discussing the history of an exercise class, something you do once or twice a week or one hour in the morning. We are talking about a state of being that is yoga, an experience which is arising from yoga and a way of life arising from that which is arising from yoga. You don't say that you are bringing your bicycle and the wheels. It is understood that if you have a bicycle, it has wheels. Yoga from a yogi's perspective is yoga as a whole, as life. And life is happening now. And now. And now. And now. That is why the first sutra in Patanjali's great work is Atha yoganushasanam, 'atha' meaning Now. Although he was writing several millennia ago, everything contained within the Yoga Sutras means as much now, today, as it did then. That is part of their brilliance. There is not a wasted word in Patanjali's teachings. All of it is relevant which is why he starts with the word Now; it is there for a purpose. It means that it doesn't matter at which point in time one is living, yoga is always relevant Now. That is the great beauty of the sutras and why this wonderful tradition of yoga has survived, has adapted, and continued. Yoga is relevant Now and forever. In the 4th century BCE, yoga is relevant Now. In the 15th century CE, yoga is relevant Now. In the 21st century, in 2050, when is it relevant? Now. Atha yoga anushasanam. Now yoga. When is Now? All centuries are Now. They are all expressions of Now.

The word yoga is Sanskrit for union, the practice of which enables one to achieve unity consciousness. Yoga stands for the state, the experience and the practice of unity. Through the state, the experience and the practice of yoga, one can transcend and evolve beyond the limitations of one's present level of existence. It helps us to refine our intellect and correct it, to become a witness to our thoughts, actions and our ego, and so to master our mind. We are not our thoughts. The way we live our lives, the way we see things, the way we impact society, all can be positively influenced by the knowledge and practice of yoga.

From a historical perspective, yoga began in the Indian subcontinent. This body of knowledge already existed long before it was written down, taught first in the oral tradition to preserve the spiritual teachings. Yogis still have an oral tradition, not everything is written down so there is still an element of secrecy to some practices. But here we are talking about the surviving literature, the oldest of which are the Vedas, ancient texts written in Sanskrit.

The Vedas are a collection of philosophical science, a library of wisdom giving us clues into the nature of reality. They were not composed by one individual. They were created through a collaboration of authors, Veda Vyasa. Vyasa is a sort of title meaning someone who has become intimate with knowledge, Veda means knowledge. So it is like the word Buddha, which also became a title for the awakened one or enlightened one. Veda Vyasa was somebody who was intimate with the Vedas. There is much discussion over the dates of these writings. Western scholars have arbitrarily chosen this date as 1500-1000 BCE, but from the Indian scholarly standpoint, and from my own research, the Vedas date back as early as 6000 BCE. The oldest of these known texts is Rig Veda, followed by Yajur Veda, Sama Veda and Atharva Veda. The word yoga had already started to be used. It appears in Rig Veda, a whole treatise that is fundamentally dealing with life in its entirety, starting with Who am I? That is a question as relevant today as it was 10,000 years ago and will still be relevant in 5,000 years. Who am I? Why am I here? What am I doing? It is that questioning about our very existence, our desire to know what it all means, which gave birth to yoga. All the Vedas are addressing these questions as well as much more, the search for the meaning of life, for a purpose. So Vedic Yoga is the practice of this knowledge. They are two sides of the same coin. Yoga is an expression of Veda and Veda is the manifestation of Yoga. The Vedas discuss how to refine this value of life more and more, moving toward inner wisdom, self-realization, and unity between our true Self and all else.

The Brahmanas start to arrive next and were written in Sanskrit. They were slightly more concise in their scope than the Vedas. They were commentaries, aids to understanding the Vedas and the specific rituals, the proper pronunciations, intonations, and hand movements. You see, it is important to realize that the rituals in the Vedas are not based on belief. The Vedas are not religious texts, they contain specific techniques developed to create a shift within oneself and they need to be understood and performed correctly. For example, if you are doing a Havan, a fire ceremony, there is a certain hypnotic effect that starts to happen, a certain meditativeness that starts to occur; these rituals are extensions of meditation. The Brahmanas, therefore, contain incredible detail about the rituals. This is not the dogmatic aspect of ritual, but ritual as in how to work with the elements, the five great elements of earth, water, fire, air and ether, and how to gain their support and balance them within the body. The Brahmanas overlapped with Atharva Veda, the last of the Vedas in linear time. So we have the latter part of the Atharva Veda, and the Brahmanas, teaching us how to balance the elements using Vedic mantras, bija mantras and discussing the use of herbs, which then gave rise to Ayurveda. This is the oldest tradition of holistic healing practiced in the world, existing for 5000 years, and it is right there in the Vedas. Again, we are talking about the whole. Ayurveda recognizes health as the harmony of mind and body, the senses and the soul. It does not treat only one aspect, Ayurveda is deeply rooted in the wisdom of nature.

After the Brahmanas, we have the Aranyakas, texts expounding on mantras, including the bija mantras, and explaining the hidden meaning in the Vedas. It is now that the first concept starts to show up of a personal god, a deity that is related to as a person. Before that we only find a force or an Absolute in the Vedas, an impersonal god. In the

Aranyakas it's the first time the Sanskrit word Ishta appears, or what Patanjali later, in the Yoga Sutras, calls god, Ishvara.

The fourth aspect of the Vedas is the Upanishads, or Vedanta, meaning the end of the Vedas, the end of knowledge, because they are discussing the nature of Self and the nature of reality. As the yogis say, "Know that by knowing which everything else is known." Once you begin to know yourself, all knowledge starts to come. That is the fundamental message of the Upanishads, the Jnana yoga, the realization of one's Self. There are many, many books within the Upanishads. The agreed number is 108, basically because it sounds nice, but in actual fact there are a lot more. A body of profound knowledge, some are extremely technical and read more like a science manual than a piece on spirituality. This is the closest thing you can find to quantum physics. So when Buddha is talking about the nature of emptiness or the nature of reality, this is all from the Upanishads, it is all Vedantic teachings. Today, when people talk about being in the moment or the power of now, this too, is all taken from the Vedantic teaching found in the Upanishads.

From the Upanishads, we move to the great Puranas, eulogizing various deities through divine stories; Ramayana, one of the largest ancient epics, is where we find Hanuman and the legendary Prince Rama who struggles to rescue his wife, Sita, and the magnificent Mahabharata, all wonderful stories. Together, they form the Itihasa, in Sanskrit literally, 'that's what happened'. This is all long before the sutras were written down, that comes much later. That is why it is amusing to hear Patanjali referred to by some as the founder of yoga. It's like saying that Einstein was the founder of science, there is simply no logic behind such a statement. So now we have the Mahabharata and Ramayana. The Puranic period was really the start of a very fertile, creative time. The wonderfully poetic Mahabharata, being seven times the length of the Iliad and the Odyssey combined, contains within it what is considered the biggest scripture of contemporary times about yoga, the Bhagavad Gita. A narrative between the Prince Arjuna and Lord Krishna, this divine conversation is a true source of spiritual knowledge that sets out to reveal the purpose of human existence. It deals with the four classical yogas of lifestyle, giving it a very distinct identity. Jnana yoga, the yoga of knowledge, which is correcting one's intellect and the way we see the world, because that is fundamentally how we shape the world, in direct alignment to the way we see it. The second being Bhakti yoga, devotion, divine love, the love of one's Self as a universal Being and connecting to the Divine through the heart. Third is Karma yoga, the yoga of right action, of service and ritual. It does not mean doing charity work. Karma yoga means our whole life is service, aligning our outer lives with the inner reality that we access through knowledge and devotion. The fourth is Raja yoga, Raja meaning royal. Ultimately, through the practice of yoga, you come into your own royal nature; that is one of the invitations of yoga, to come into your own Self, transcend your own victim identity. One of the great assault weapons of the ego is to slide into victimhood, which is extremely infectious; it can stick not only to individuals but also cultures, communities, races. That then becomes part of their narrative, that victim story. So Raja as a word means transcendence of the victim identity and is the yoga of meditation. There are four distinct types of yoga but not four distinct paths. They may appear to all be different on the surface but as you go deeper, Krishna makes this very clear, when you practice one you will start to realize that they cannot exist in isolation. They have to exist in togetherness, practiced as a whole.

Following the Puranas, we have the birth of Tantra as a distinct movement. I say distinct because it is important to realize that already in the Vedas there is Tantra. This is not the populist, modern misunderstanding of Tantra as something just to do with sex. This is the ancient, powerful practice combining mantra, mudra, asana, bandha, and chakra work. The Vedas discuss both the chakras and shakti, the divine energy. Tan in Sanskrit means energy, and tra means expansion. Tantra means to work with the expansive potential of energy. After the Upanishads, these teachings start to be classified as Tantric scriptures. It is here where we see techniques being developed, practices being refined. These Tantric scriptures, also known as the Agamas, are a voluminous work, they are as big as the Vedas and Upanishads combined.

Now we come to Patanjali's Yoga Sutras. Here he is fundamentally discussing meditation on the level of technique, it's Raja yoga, the yoga of meditation. There is a difference of opinion as to the exact period in which Patanjali lived, but from the viewpoint of the yogis, it was around the 4th to 5th century BCE, again a very fertile time. The Buddha's teachings came about around this time and all the big names start to appear. There was a great concentration of geniuses. Patanjali, Buddha, Mahavira, Lao Tsu, Confucius and the Hellenic philosophers, Socrates and Aristotle, were all born in the same era. Surely this suggests that there was something rather magical going on, on Earth at that time. There are two other works attributed to Patanjali about which scholars argue, one being a treatise on Sanskrit grammar and the other a treatise on Ayurveda. Arguing seems to be the nature of scholars, but we are not interested in arguments. What we are interested in is the great gift Patanjali offers in his 196 yoga sutras. He stays true to the essence of yoga not only in his practice, but also in his writing. In this masterwork, he mentions Kriya yoga twice as being an instrument through which human evolution can be quickened, and says that it consists of body discipline, mental control and meditating on AUM. He talks about god as the actual cosmic sound of AUM heard in meditation.

Simultaneously Tantra is on the increase, but it is important to remember that Tantra is a collective term, just as Vedic is also a collective term. Tantra does not exist in isolation because that would have no meaning. The Tantric scriptures, also known as Agamas, start to explode because they are freeing spirituality from the corruption of the teachings, which naturally occurs over time. Now the mantras start to be much more precise, the bija mantras are much clearer and we start to talk about the deities too. They start to be mentioned in the Tantric scriptures where specific rituals, specific practices, specific meditations are now being written about. This is where we first hear the word Kundalini, the rising of an energy and consciousness which has been coiled at the base of the spine since birth. In the Vedas before this, it is the Sanskrit word 'Kundal', meaning the crooked or coiled one, and is the practice of how to tap into the infinite potential of Being, later becoming Kundalini yoga. When they wrote about it originally, it wasn't called that. When they wrote about the power of sound, they didn't call it Nada yoga. When they talk about using the breath and activating certain aspects within oneself, they didn't call it Kriya. Later these words start to be given to certain practices and techniques, and then more and more is written about them.

That, in linear time, is how yoga evolved as a holistic practice encompassing all aspects of life, all aspects of the mind and the body. Nothing was separate from the whole. Meditation was not a mindfulness class you did on a Wednesday evening. It was how you lived your life. But as with many things in the move from East to West, much has been lost in translation. In the early 1890s, Swami Vivekananda first travelled to America to represent India and Hinduism at the Parliament of the World's Religions in Chicago. An eloquent young man in his early 30s from a very wealthy family in Calcutta, Swami Vivekananda soon caught the imagination of the Americans. He was dynamic, a very well-educated, intellectual guy. A wonderful speaker with a vast knowledge of both Eastern and Western culture he was deeply spiritual and insightful. It is said that no one could forget him once they had heard him speak and his fame spread quickly. You see, with his flowing robes and air of mysticism, he had the whole Jesus thing going for him, and then of course, the floodgates opened. In 1920, Paramahansa Yogananda, the great genius, went to America and founded the Self-Realization Fellowship. He wrote his incredible book, Autobiography of a Yogi, which has been reprinted endlessly and read by all, from yogis to priests, and CEOs to shop assistants. It is considered a spiritual classic. The Beatle, George Harrison, was known to have carried a bag filled with copies to give away. When he wrote the song, My Sweet Lord, he changed the word Hallelujah to Hare Krishna halfway through, so that people would be singing the Maha Mantra without even knowing it. Steve Jobs was also a big fan, he read it every year and had copies handed out to those who attended his memorial.

Of course, it was in the 1960s that yoga took another leap, when we had the great explosion of psychedelic drugs which opened up the minds and all sorts of possibilities to many people in the West. People started to question what they were doing and why they were doing it; they chose spiritually based practices rather than conventional religions, read the Bhagavad Gita and took pilgrimages to India. It is interesting that the West's first interaction with yoga, in India, was a spiritual one. The people who came back from their travels in India at that time, and all the people who have been on the yogic path for over twenty years, will all have had a much greater spiritual understanding of yoga than those who are starting yoga now. That is just the way of things. All movements have four cycles to them, the first being the innovators, then the early adopters, the early majority, and finally the late majority.

Yoga is now at the late majority stage. It is growing at an exponential rate and any movement which gathers that speed is bound to have its original meaning distorted. This happens over and over again with any movement. It is the nature of evolution that things change. There will always be innovators that emerge to refine, add something new and put it back together again.

An Introduction to Patanjali and the Yoga Sutras

Patanjali was an illuminated being and a yogi, established in the state, the practice and the experience of yoga. He wrote the Yoga Sutras to be as relevant today as they were when they were first created. Written in a time when there were no printing presses, no publishers, no paperback or hardcovers, no self-help genres, no bookstores, Kindle E-readers or eBooks, no Booker Prize or Pulitzers to aim for, he clearly did not put these teachings down on paper out of any desire for worldly recognition. He was a great practitioner as well as being a master of the word. But the Yoga Sutras were not written by a scholar. Patanjali was a yogi first and a writer second, a master of yoga trying to share his experience. This great work arose from a state of consciousness that was deeply in tune with the state, practice and experience of yoga. It arose out of compassion, as a service to his fellow beings. In the sutras he explains that yoga is an evolutionary way of life and he offers us an invitation, a key, to a portal of altered consciousness, where you have access to a clearer perception.

The word Patanjali is really a title. He probably wasn't called this at the time. In Sanskrit, Patalika means the knower of secrets, the one who lifts the veil on that which is hidden. He lights the fire, ignites the passion for the unknown. Also called a Rishi or Seer, one who has a corrected perception, one who is not deluded anymore, Patanjali has, over time, taken on an almost mythical quality. In certain traditions of yoga he is considered half-snake, half-man, but this is more a symbolic representation of the sage. The serpent symbolizes potential, because his teachings give us access to the potential of being and in the yogic tradition the potential of being, which is also called Kundalini, is often expressed as a coiled serpent. So that is why he is often depicted as half-snake, half-man and is considered an incarnation of Vishnu. Why Vishnu? Because it means the sustainer. He is the organizing, sustaining power of the universe. When the individual really gets intimate with the knowledge of the Yoga Sutras, then they have an infinite power to sustain bliss consciousness, meaning the deep inner state of existential joy, in this dimension of reality and beyond.

As mentioned earlier, there is a difference of opinion as to the exact period that Patanjali lived, but most yogis agree that he must have existed around the 4th to 5th century BCE. As I have previously said, if we look at this period in linear time, there was a concentration of geniuses, so something really quite magical was going on, on Earth during this period. Patanjali was very well aware, in his realized state, that scholars would fight over what time period the Yoga Sutras were written, that they may be seen as some kind of antiquity and could be said not to be relevant. But that is the brilliance of the Yoga Sutras. Unlike some religious scriptures which sound comical because they don't fit into the consciousness of our contemporary times, don't have any relevance and to which we are not very receptive, the Yoga Sutras have more relevance now than ever before. It's quite fascinating that even back in medieval times in India, although they were translated into 400 languages or more, the Yoga Sutras were not as popular as they are now. They were well read but then faded for a while, until in the 8th century Adi Guru Shankaracharya wrote a treatise, a commentary, on them and the rise in interest in them grew. The next time they were popular was in the 14th and 15th centuries. But their popularity really grew in the 20th century after Swami Vivekananda brought them to America. The sutras become more and more relevant over time. A lot of historical scriptures tend to lose their relevance because they speak in a certain manner and of certain concepts which seem very alien to us. But not the Yoga Sutras. They have gained greater and greater relevance, greater and greater importance, have had greater and greater reception as we have come into modern times.

Why is that? Why are these 196 poetic verses still so relevant? This is one of the most translated works arising out of India. Why? Because it arose from a state of consciousness which was in yoga. Meaning that the individual, Patanjali, was not merely a writer writing to an audience. He was not writing to be sold in bookshops. He was a yogi teaching the Yoga Sutras to yogis, beings who were practicing, who were interested in the whole art and science of liberation. It was an art and it was a science. That science was relevant then, and that science is relevant now.

Patanjali was clearly very logical in his approach to the Yoga Sutras. There is a wonderful poetry to his work because obviously at the time when he was sharing these teachings, there were no means of mass publishing, so their poetic design would have enabled them to be shared orally far more easily. He was very logical about this design. When you read the sutras, you can dissect every step. They are clear and precise and really lay out yoga as a science. But the manner in which they are laid out is an art. It is not just an intellectual, dry, scientific treatise; it is an incredible piece of poetry. Such is his genius throughout the sutras. Patanjali stays true to the whole essence of yoga, uniting Shiva and Shakti, the yin and the yang. It is clear that this being was vibrating at a state synonymous with yoga, with unity consciousness, meaning to unite us to our true Selves and all others. And he does all this in such a precise manner using just 196 sutras over four padas, or books.

The Yoga Sutras are the threads of wisdom Patanjali offers us as guidelines. If this magnificent body of knowledge is truly appreciated and practiced, then it is the manual on how to live an authentic, meaningful life. He outlines the eight limbs of yoga, and over the 196 sutras, he concisely and clearly explains how the nature of Self, the nature of Being, is pure consciousness. Such is the precision in Patanjali's writing that he does not waste a single word as he ties these threads together in an impeccable garland and presents it to humanity.

What is also remarkable about the Yoga Sutras is that although it is an ancient scripture, it does not ask its reader, practitioner or student to have any belief. It is not a scripture based in religion. It does not demand an individual to have faith in something. It does not tell a mythological story. Through its poetry, it is an incredibly clear, concise, and systematic approach to the question of existence. Who are we? How can we realize our essential nature and our purpose here in this world? Patanjali spent his life answering these questions, which in itself is an incredible practice of yoga.

There are only four padas in the Yoga Sutras. The first is Samadhi, the second is Sadhana, the third is Vibhuti, and the fourth is Kaivalya. Just four padas and 196 sutras. He did not write 1000. He did not write 1200. He wrote 196. So every sutra here is loaded and contains a totality, a whole, within each one. This is the brilliance of his work. This brings us to the meaning of word sutra. There are, of course, several meanings. Patanjali's work is multi-layered, the depth contained in the sutras is huge. You cannot translate them, you can only interpret them. He wants us to explore the meaning, but that meaning does not remain static, it is dynamic. The first meaning is an unbroken chain. You see, Patanjali's Sutras cannot be approached in isolation, they should be seen as a whole. By calling his work the Yoga Sutras, Patanjali warns the human mind against the tendency for it to reduce, to be reductionist and separatist. The human mind by its very nature is reductionist, it reduces knowledge, it compartmentalizes and isolates one piece of knowledge from another. This is not the yogic approach, and not Patanjali's approach; his is a whole, organic approach. Each piece of knowledge has a deeper understanding and relevance when connected with others. They can be grouped together to gain this deeper understanding. So when you really begin to look at the whole 196 sutras, you really see this complete picture. Not complete in a sense that it is static, but complete meaning it is whole and it is also evolving. This whole body of knowledge is evolving.

Sutra also means a key to opening up an expanded state of consciousness. A key is very small; take this key to a door, open it, and this tiny key opens the way to an incredible palace inside. The sutras are also a clue to guide us toward treasure. As we all know, the best treasure hunts have complex clues. You have to really commit to the search and work hard to find the treasure. So when you really enter into the meaning of the Yoga Sutras, when you really go deep into them, not just the meaning as expressed by the words, but as intended by the state of consciousness through which they are being shared, then you have access to a deeper realm of consciousness. Each sutra acts as a clue to our evolution, a key to open doorways to subtler perceptions. That is Patanjali's approach to yoga. It is not putting your right leg behind your neck. That is not Patanjali's yoga. Patanjali's yoga is the art and science of transforming oneself and reaching one's true potential in a very deep manner, expanding one's consciousness and transforming one's being. He teaches yoga as an evolutionary, integrated way of life, not merely body culture. That is absolutely not Patanjali's intention and he makes that very clear. It is important to keep these multiple meanings of sutra in our consciousness.

The aim here is to show how padas one and two of Patanjali's Yoga Sutras are as relevant for today as ever and to integrate our yoga practice into our modern lives, as laid down by the great Seer. We must stay consistent with our practice, with the techniques, both within and without, in its fullest value. Now, naturally, if you are consistent with your practice, pay attention to your state of consciousness and align yourself with the laws of nature, then there will be an expansion of your consciousness, a refinement of your nervous system, of your intellect. That only occurs when the practice of yoga is at its fullest value. This consistency is key. When this consistency is done in the correct manner, is cultivated in the holistic manner, the practice ends because it is no longer a practice. It is just an expression of who you are. Then the practice is not a separate thing you do, not a means to an end. Instead, you are the practice.

You will find you have an optimal amount of energy and are working at your fullest capacity. Less knowledge in an individual makes them very noisy, loudness is a clear sign of a lack of knowledge. Like the weak current in the motor of a fan makes it noisy, as does too much current, but when there is the optimal current the fan works perfectly and in silence. It is doing the same work but with the optimal current, it is not disturbing you. Ignorant people, where disharmony is dominating in them, will do their work but they will make sure everybody knows about it, they will talk about it. But when wise people are busy, you will not even know about it. The greater the value of wisdom in you, the greater impact you have but with less noise. The less wisdom in you, the less impact, but there is more noise, just like the fan. These days, people are very noisy about what they are up to. They're very keen to let everyone know, but they don't accomplish anything. They have no impact, their service is always an agenda. The people in real service, who are really devoted, are not noisy about it. They just get on with it, and their service has such fragrance, there is no noise there.

It is important to remember that whatever state you approach anything, that will be the aspect that is revealed back to you. If you approach this moment with arrogance or aggression, this moment will reveal that aspect to you. If you approach this very moment with receptivity, devotion and deep appreciation, then these aspects will shine most brilliantly in your consciousness. Therefore, I invite you all to enter the Yoga Sutras in a state of deep reverence and receptivity. In a state of gratefulness to all the Masters who came before us and dedicated their lives to sharing this magnificent body of knowledge with us which, if really and truly appreciated and practiced, can solve all the problems of humanity.

Samadhi Pada

unity

The first book of the Yoga Sutras is Samadhi pada. It is a very important point here, the first pada of the sutras is not practice. It is not Sadhana; it is Samadhi, which means unity, the same name as the last limb in Patanjali's Eight Limbs of Yoga. The beginning of the Yoga Sutras is also where the Yoga Sutras end. Beginning and end stay together. His approach is not linear; it's a holistic, organic approach. The Eight Limbs of Yoga are called Ashtanga, anga meaning limbs. The eight limbs are Yama, Niyama, Asana, Pranayama, Pratyahara, Dharana, Dhyana and Samadhi. Samadhi is the ultimate state. Yet it is the first book of the Yoga Sutras. Look at the brilliance of this piece of work, the genius of Patanjali. He is clearly declaring to us that the Ashtanga is not eight steps to yoga, they are the eight aspects of yoga, aspects of a being who is in the state of yoga. Our limbs are not steps to our body. My right arm or my left leg is not a step to my body. Like my right hand, my left hand is an expression of my body. They are a part of my body as a whole. Ashtanga is often wrongly translated as eight steps of yoga when in actual fact, they are the eight aspects, the eight expressions, of yoga. We have to approach them all at once, as a whole, not in a linear progression. They are inseparable and for a being to be in the state of yoga, he has to be vibrating in all eight aspects.

That Patanjali used the word samadhi is a brilliant piece of creativity. Samadhi means to unify, to be absorbed into the whole. Ego is separation. Samadhi is unity. Why do we have all these problems in our life? This violence in our world? Because human beings have become stuck in a state of isolation, separate from the whole, stuck in an egotistical, myopic worldview dominated by 'me' in isolation. A me which is in conflict with the whole, a me which is primarily concerned with its own survival, a me whose base is fear. What Patanjali is saying here is, as we enter this scripture, if we are truly interested in the art and science of yoga, then we have to let go of me. It's a clear invitation to drop our ego and enter these yoga sutras from a state of unity consciousness, to realize that we are not separate from the whole. To realize that we are not our ego or our body, not just the ideas floating around in our head, not just the sum total of our whole experience, not just our memory, but that there is something within us that is far greater. It is the silent one that has never spoken a word, the witness within you which exists beyond the domain of time.

Patanjali is showing us that these practices and techniques of yoga are going to allow us to experience that which is already here. It's not somewhere else. The practice of yoga is not to take you from here to a distant future, millions and millions of light years away, in some kind of fluffy cloud, filled with angels and celestial music, where you will live for eternity, happily ever after. That is not the view of a world Patanjali wants to share with us, an escapist view. He is sharing something which is very realistic, something clear and whole. So by naming the first book Samadhi, he invites us to pause, to acknowledge what state of consciousness we are approaching it in. Not with an egotistical mindset, still trying to gain knowledge to prepare a better mask for itself, but rather as a being who is deeply eager to realize his or her own unity, eager to move toward unity, not toward greater and greater separation. Moving toward unity is moving toward love, moving with love, moving through love. Moving toward separation, moving toward isolation, toward me, me, me, is the ego moving through fear.

So here, in the Yoga Sutras, is an invitation to move through love to love from love. As the great sutra says, you exist through love, you come through love and ultimately unto love you shall return. In contemporary times, Samadhi pada could be entitled, Love. Look at the brilliance of it. samadhi meaning total absorption, total unity, where the dominant experience of the individual is of unity, which is love. That is what love is. We find points of unification, how we are connected, how we are similar, how you see me, and how I see you, and I start seeing myself in you, and you start seeing yourself in me. And there is the birth of love. You realize that ultimately you and I are not separate, we are reflections of that one whole, this idea of separation is only on the surface.

LOVE IS

Ultimately there is just the Self. That is love. That you are love, I am love, everything is love. That is Samadhi. This knowledge can at least dominate the level of your intellect and when it starts to dominate, the knowledge itself starts to correct the intellect. Because the intellect needs to be corrected. Patanjali is a very intellectual guy. He knows you cannot kick out intellect and totally dumb it all down. That is why yoga is a holistic practice; it includes our intellect, refines it and then transcends it. So, here in the Samadhi pada, love and unity consciousness are dominating. Now you can approach it from that place where you are love, experiencing love, and allowing love that is loving you. You are not entering the Yoga Sutras from a place of fear, from a place of dogma or a false belief system, hoping to find something that will take you to a magical heaven. No, you are approaching it as a yogi, to realize what is here inside you already and to refine your understanding and perception of that.

अथ योगानुशासनम् ॥ १ ॥

1:1 Atha yoganushasanam

A lot of interpreters of Patanjali's work just skim over this first sutra, but that's a big mistake. It completely misses his genius because right here, in the very first sutra, he says atha meaning now. Now yoga. Now yoga is explained. Now yoga is experienced. Now yoga is practiced. When? Now. Right at the outset Patanjali is declaring that yoga can only happen Now. Yoga can only be understood Now. Yoga can only be practiced Now. You can only experience yoga Now. You can only talk about yoga Now. You can never approach yoga tomorrow. Or yesterday. Or 500 days from now. Atha yoganushasanam. Yoga is to be practiced, experienced and realized. When? Now. Look at the brilliance of it. It does not matter when the Yoga Sutras were written because whenever you approach them, it's Now.

As already discussed, from the yogic perspective the domain of time is merely a scholarly debate, for the yogi it doesn't matter when the Yoga Sutras were written, in the 4th century or just one week ago. It's not relevant for a being who is practicing, who is sincerely interested in the science and art of yoga as a liberating piece of knowledge. For someone who is merely reading it as an entertainment, then yes, they might well be very interested in when it was written and want to argue about it, but that is to miss the whole point of what Patanjali is saying. The Yoga Sutras begin at whatever dimension of time you are in. He is stating the universality of this knowledge. This knowledge is relevant irrespective of which era you are in, which dimension of the space-time continuum. The teachings of yoga are always relevant. They are relevant anytime and anywhere. Atha yoganushasanam. When? Now. The 1st century is

Now. The 21st century is Now. They are all expressions of Now. From the outset, Patanjali, the seer, the great sage, destroys the whole concept of time. So to dismiss this as him merely saying the Yoga Sutras begin, is to misunderstand his genius and the incredible power of this first sutra. If you are asking Patanjali, when will I reach the state of yoga? His answer is atha, Now. When will suffering end? Now. When will I find bliss? Now. This is his brilliance. Be in a state of yoga Now. Practice yoga Now. Experience yoga Now.

योगश्चित्तवृत्तिनिरोधः ॥ २ ॥

1:2 Yogash chitta vritti nirodhah

Patanjali gives us an incredibly powerful key here to an expanded consciousness, when he says, yoga is the cessation of the modification of consciousness. If you just took these first two sutras alone you could have satori, the Zen word for samadhi. You could have samadhi. When? Now.

Patanjali says our essential nature, the nature of who we are, is pure consciousness, infinite consciousness, chitta, what in yoga we refer to as sat chit ananda. That is the true nature of Self. Sat is unchanging. It is beyond the domain of time. It includes all variables of time yet transcends them. It is not relative, it has an absolute quality to it. Sat Chit, pure consciousness, it is alive. Conscious, meaning it is alert, it is aware, it is not inert. Our essential nature is unbounded awareness. Ananda, bliss. Sat chit ananda. The essential nature of Self is sat chit ananda, is bliss. The nature of consciousness is infinite because everything is consciousness. That is the yogic view, that consciousness is all there is. All things are consciousness arising from one unified whole, the self-aware unified field.

What is the first modification of consciousness? The first disturbance of consciousness? There is, of course, a multi-layered meaning here. Remember, when we approach these sutras there is never just one meaning. The fundamental meaning here, the powerful meaning, is that the first modification of consciousness, or disturbance of consciousness, is the sense of I am-ness. I am Indian. I am American. I am man. I am woman. I am a failure. I am successful. I am fat. I am skinny. I am this. I am that. Nobody likes me. Everybody likes me. People are jealous of me. People don't like me. Everybody should love me. Nobody loves me. Me, me, me. I, I, I. Me, I, me, I. One's whole universe is within the context of this me, I, me which is in isolation. Patanjali says when this illusion of the self as an isolated entity ceases, then that is yoga. The state where this individual realizes that ultimately it does not exist.

What does exist, Patanjali says, is totality, the whole. Therefore, the individualized expression of that only exists in the context of that, not in isolation from consciousness. When this I wakes up to that realization, this I am-ness is not a disturbance anymore. It's not a vritti. Vritti is not just merely a modification, it means a deformation. Vritti in Sanskrit means something which is deformed, not vibrating in an intelligent manner. Here, vritti means a modification of consciousness in an unintelligent manner. When this modification of consciousness in an unintelligent manner ceases, then that is yoga. What is this unintelligent modification of consciousness? Ego, the sense of I as separate from the whole, separate from consciousness. The sense of I which is fundamentally anchored in the body, that I am just this body and I begin and end here, and my sense of self only extends through what I own, through what has happened to me. Patanjali is saying that the realization of this knowledge can dawn on us right now, chitta vritti nirodhah, we can experience it right now. This is the beauty of yoga. Atha yoganushasanam, chitta vritti nirodhah. Right now, we can experience the ending of the unintelligent modification of our essential nature.

Our essential nature is what? Chitta, pure consciousness. Stretched to infinity in all directions, right now. You are not just your body. You are not just your story. You are not just your skin color. You are not just your nationality. You are not just the collection of memories that is held in your nervous system. You are beyond that. So if you can let go of this obsession with I, this unintelligent modification of consciousness, then that is the beginning of yoga; the state of yoga, the practice of yoga and the experience of yoga.

What is the state of yoga? Chitta vritti. Pure consciousness. The practice of yoga is this realization, this act of observing. You can observe that you are not merely the wave arising from the ocean, you are the wave and you are the ocean, together. This awareness then starts to dominate your consciousness. Now you are the ocean and not just obsessing about the wave. As you begin to observe the ocean, the value of the ocean begins to dominate your awareness and your consciousness begins to expand; vritti nirodhah, the value of infinite consciousness starts to dominate the value of self.

The other meaning is the cessation of thought. As the individual practices meditation, asana, pranayama, dharana and dhyana, the cessation of thought starts to happen. Then the yogi starts to gather perception beyond thought. That too is yoga. When you start to achieve the level of pure consciousness, the mind starts to return to the source. Instead of being constantly directed in an external direction, going outward, it starts to turn inside, within itself. Now the movement is not external, the thoughts are not moving in from an outward direction. They have ceased, but the attention is there. Now the attention starts to move in a totally different direction away from thought. It starts to move within itself. The awareness starts to move within itself. Now the object drops and is replaced by the subject and the subject starts to become the object. That is yoga. That is self-realization.

तदा द्रष्टुः स्वरूपेऽवस्थानम् ॥ ३ ॥

1:3 Tada drashtuh svarupe avasthanam

What happens when chitta vritti nirodhah occurs? Patanjali explains it all brilliantly in the third sutra: Then the seer's perception corrects itself. As the disturbance of consciousness ceases and the light of consciousness starts to dominate, and is no longer merely object-focused, then the nervous system starts to refine. As the nervous system becomes refined, it starts to reflect the total value of consciousness, not just the reductionist value. Then the seer starts to see his or her own true nature, tada drashtuh svarupe avasthanam. The seer starts to not only see their own nature but to also reside in their own nature. Which is what? Chitta, pure consciousness. When will this happen? Atha, Now.

As you practice, when you let go of the obsession with the unintelligent modification of consciousness, with the illusion of a separate self, then naturally and spontaneously you will start to catch a glimpse of your essential nature, of the light of consciousness. You will come face to face with the reality of who you are and not of some false identity, some alien entity, but of your essential nature, this incredible love. What is the first book called? Samadhi. Here Patanjali is describing the most intimate love affair. This incredible love affair. The witnessing of truth. The witnessing of the essential nature of Self. Tada drashtuh svarupe avasthanam. The seer sees their own nature. They reside in their own nature. They start to get settled in their own nature and their perception is corrected. The quality of our perception is limited by our nervous system. When your eyes see your hand, your nervous system collects data and creates a picture, an identity of who you are, who you think you are, all based on the data collected by the organs of perception. But through the practice of yoga, the nervous system is refined and the organs of perception no longer limit that which we perceive. Patanjali says that when these organs of perception refine, they allow the perception of the subtler aspects of self to arise in the field of our awareness, because all perception is ultimately arising from our consciousness. So as the organs of perception turn inward toward the subject and there is no longer an obsession with the object, the natural quality of perception that arises gives us the glimpse of the truth of who we are. That is the state of yoga.

वृत्तिसारूप्यम् इतरत्र ॥ ४ ॥

1:4 *Vritti saroopyam itaratra*

When we, the individual expression of the indivisible whole, the small self, are not in the state of yoga, and are not witnessing our own essential nature, then we are identifying with the fluctuations of consciousness and so are bound by ignorance. Here, Patanjali creates a clear distinction between the state of yoga and the state of non-yoga. The state of non-yoga is a state of ego-dominated consciousness and is bound by the ego identity, bound by this entity encased in a bag of skin. When the awareness is dominated by this ego, is in isolation and is not seeing one's essential nature, then one is attached or identified with the fluctuations of the mind, with every small wave arising out of the consciousness. Now be with that for a while. It's profound.

What Patanjali is clearly saying here is that either you are free or you are bound in bondage. But in the state of yoga, where you can see your essential nature, you are witnessing your essential nature, which is infinite consciousness. At that level you and I are one. Even though our bodies are separate and in different locations in the space-time continuum, all of us exist within the field of consciousness. You all exist in my field of consciousness and I exist within the field of your consciousness. As we go to a subtler level, we find the surface value of the manifest reality is fluctuating and ever-changing, but behind this fluctuating is the unchanging whole that is our essential nature. This body is not the primary Self. This body is actually the secondary self. The sense of Self comes before the body. You see, the body has been changing over time, the story of this body, the story of who we think we are, but the sense of I am-ness has continued. The I am-ness is immortal and so is the Is-ness. The Is-ness has been here before time and the Is-ness will be here after all matter becomes emptiness. When it all dissolves into nothingness, the Is-ness will remain. The I am-ness and the Is-ness will still remain. Ultimately, the I am-ness and the Is-ness are one. What Patanjali is saying here is there will be times when the yogi is not in the state of yoga. They may be identifying with the fluctuations of consciousness. The chronic illness of humanity may be inflicted upon them, this state of self-hatred, this sense of victimhood, of not having enough. Then they have to realize that this is just a story arising from a place of identification with the small self, they are not witnessing their own true nature.

Mind you, when you do begin to witness your own true nature, the infinite nature of your Being, that does not mean that the relevant world becomes irrelevant. Far from it. You actually become more relevant in that relative field because you now begin to witness the backdrop, the unchanging whole which is behind the ever-changing surface value. It is very important to understand that as you are realizing your own true nature, when you start to really come into unity consciousness, there is a natural freedom, an inner freedom, that starts to happen. But that does not in any way, shape or form, make you turn away from the Is-ness of the manifest reality. You stay relevant in that manifest reality, only now, you are able to see beyond the surface value. As you are able to see beyond it, you are able to work within it in a more non-violent manner, a more loving manner, because you have access to the absolute value of Self, beyond the surface value. You are no longer identified with the fluctuations of the mind. All that arises from the field of consciousness no longer dominates you or your awareness. The observer is not lost in the observed. The object of your awareness, of your consciousness, is no longer able to dominate the subject. The subjective awareness of Being remains. As the subjective awareness of Being remains, then the object can be appreciated in its finite value, whatever that object may be. Therefore, you are able to have a much more optimal experience of the finite values of being, because you are able to witness the infinite value of Being.

This is what Patanjali is saying. In the state of non-yoga, the individual is only identified with the finite value, the fluctuation of consciousness. Finite because it is fluctuating, so it has a beginning, it has a peak, and it has an end. When that is your dominant identity, that is what is dominating the field of your awareness. Then you are bound by weakness, bound by fear. The dominant experience will be of anxiety, of fear, of conflict, of competitiveness, of never being enough. There will be a lot of noise, as this noise is a natural byproduct of this movement, this constant movement, because the field of your awareness will be totally consumed by the fluctuations of your consciousness. The individual won't have the capacity to respond to life because they are working within that narrow domain filled with fear and anxiety, limited by being identified with the fluctuations of consciousness.

Patanjali brilliantly juxtaposes the unity consciousness and the ego consciousness. He is not talking about being totally established in unity consciousness but rather that you are moving in that direction, moving toward yoga rather than away from yoga. Unity essentially means love, the uniting force of love. At any moment in your life you can either be moving toward unity consciousness, toward love, or you are moving away from it, toward fear, toward isolation, toward an identity which is very limited and which is increasingly stressed, increasingly isolated, burdened by the very thing it is experiencing, which is life. So as a yogi, you have to be alert in every moment of your life. Are you moving toward unity, toward yoga? Or are you moving in the opposite direction toward isolation, toward the ego identity? Are you narrowing your life, entering a little box and staying within that box? Or are you transcending all boxes? Are you breaking through all barriers and moving more and more toward an expansive state of consciousness? Are you moving toward infinity or are you moving toward limitation?

Patanjali made this very clear. Vritti saroopyam itaratra. When the being is not in the state of yoga, not moving toward the state of yoga, then they are moving toward limitation, identifying with the fluctuations of consciousness, the vritti of consciousness dominated by a conditioned identity. Be with that for a while, right now, in your consciousness.

वृत्तयः पञ्चतय्यः क्लिष्टा अक्लिष्टाः ॥ ५ ॥

1:5 Vrittayah pangchatayyah klishtaklishtah

The five vrittis, Patanjali points out, are fundamentally the thoughts floating within the field of one's consciousness. Even though the thoughts are infinite in number, he has categorized them for us in five broad categories. The boundaries of these categories are in no way rigid in their nature, as indeed none of the yogic teachings are. What Patanjali is giving us here is a tool, a viewpoint, a clear viewpoint to understand the kind of thought waves which can float within the field of consciousness. He uses the word klishtaklishtah, meaning that these vrittis, these thought waves, can be either an obstacle to the experience of yoga, helpful to the experience of yoga, or neutral to the experience of yoga. It is extremely important for us to realize that by using the word klishtaklishtah, Patanjali shows us he is speaking from an absolute state of experience here. For when we go into deep states of samadhi and are in total unity and absorption, all thought waves dissolve. Only I am-ness remains. The process of going deeper within oneself, into the great depth of silence, ultimately will give rise to a mind which is corrected, an intellect which is corrected. Thoughts which are based on correct knowledge, and not on incorrect knowledge, are serving our evolutionary process. However, for us to get to that state and to be able to increase the positive mind, a mind where the content is supportive of our evolutionary process, we must realize that all knowledge has to be transcended, because when we come into relative reality, we find this movement, these thought waves, can arise. That is why he points out these five vrittis, a broad spectrum within which all thought waves are contained, but they are klishtaklishtah. Klishta meaning obstacle and aklishtah meaning that which is not an obstacle. They can be obstacles to the experience of yoga and they can be supportive to the experience of yoga.

Klishta can also be translated as painful. So these obstacles can be painful and not painful. That which is not taking us toward the direction of yoga is ultimately painful and that activity which is based on correct knowledge is not painful. Any activity of the mind which is not based on correct knowledge gives rise to an inner struggle, inner pain. Any mental activity which is based on correct knowledge gives rise to unity.

प्रमाणविपर्ययविकल्पनिद्रास्मृतयः ॥ ६ ॥

1:6 *Pramanna viparyaya vikalpa nidra smritayah*

From sutras 6 to 11, Patanjali discusses the different mental activities, the different types of content that flow in the field of one's consciousness. He looks at the distinct modifications, or aspects, of these mental activities.

Here in sutra 6, Patanjali lists the five categories. Pramanna is insight, valid knowledge, correct knowledge, valid proof. Viparyaya, incorrect knowledge based on incorrect intellect. Vikalpa, imaginary cognition, it can also be verbal delusion or knowledge which is purely conceptual, which is not backed by the depth of the experience but is merely just the conceptual understanding, hence is incorrect. Nidra which is sleep and smritayah, recollections, memory. It is important for us to understand that what Patanjali is saying is that through yoga we want to transcend all these vrittis.

प्रत्यक्षानुमानागमाः प्रमाणानि ॥ ७॥

1:7 Pratyakshanumanagamah pramanani

Correct knowledge arises from direct perception, conclusions and learning that is coming from an illuminated source, whether it is a teacher or corrected intellect or through one's own inner depth of experience. It is important for us to understand that Patanjali is listing correct knowledge as a vritti, meaning that ultimately, through the process of yoga, we have to transcend that as well. Otherwise even correct knowledge can start to limit the jiva, the atman. He says for knowledge, even correct knowledge, to be of evolutionary help to us it must not be static. It must remain fluid and dynamic, because the nature of the universe is infinite, so that knowledge can never reach an end. Through the practice of yoga, as we transcend, this correct knowledge will only increase in us. It is important for us to realize though, that even when we favor correct knowledge which arises through direct perception, inference, correct listening and studying, it is dynamic in nature, it has to be refined. For if this correct knowledge is experienced as static, it loses its relevance and starts to become stale.

So this sutra's purpose is twofold. First, to remind us that correct knowledge is that which arises within us through direct experience or from a reliable source. Secondly, and here's the trick you see, to remind us that a listener listens from their state of consciousness. Meaning the knowledge that is floating in the field of our awareness only has the value of the level that our consciousness is at. We may favor correct knowledge but in yoga we transcend all knowledge, even that which is backed by rational logic, so that it does not become a prison which keeps us limited in our self-righteousness. It's natural though that through the practice, and applying our experience of samadhi, of unity consciousness, we will find that our mental activity has a greater content of pramanna. Meaning that as the intellect gets corrected, the content becomes more and more based on correct knowledge. Correct knowledge by its essential nature is illuminating. It moves us in the direction of expansion, transcends pain, and has the quality of resolving the inner crisis. Incorrect knowledge keeps us in a state of crisis within ourselves. As this correct knowledge increases in us we find that we are able to verify it within our own experience, and not through others, as it will have the fragrance of supreme truth.

विपर्ययो मिथ्याज्ञानम् अतद्रूपप्रतिष्ठम् ॥ ८ ॥

1:8 Viparyayo mithyajnanam atadroopapratishtham

Here, Patanjali is talking about incorrect knowledge, another mental activity. Viparyayo meaning incorrect, mithya meaning false. False conclusion, false knowledge, that we may find what shows up as knowledge is actually an error in perception. In Sanskrit, we call it pragya aparadh, the crime of the intellect. Where we are bound by an incorrect perception of the Is-ness, yet because the individual is experiencing this incorrect perception, they are confused and take this incorrect perception as correct. Hence, this is a klishta, a vritti which is a klishta; it is a hindrance to our evolution. This mental activity, these thought waves, do not have anything to do with reality, they have a foundation in incorrect knowledge, in ignorance. So these thoughts and perceptions which arise from this field of ignorance are interfering with our evolution. We can see that when we are bound by these waves of mithyajnanam rising within us, they will create conflict and an experience of limitation, an experience of isolation, an experience of weakness, within ourself. They will take us away from the experience of yoga. The classic example is when the senses perceive a rope but think that it is a snake. That is a viparyaya, meaning it is incorrect knowledge but it has created fear within you. It is about perceiving reality and assuming it is static, about seeing shapes and forms and believing that boundaries are definitive. We believe these boundaries are definitive because it is proved by our senses which tell us so, yet we know that there are no boundaries really. Boundaries are not definitive. Science has verified this for us. They are merely the five sensory experience. Yet if our whole understanding of reality is fundamentally based on that, that is viparyayo, incorrect knowledge, then the thoughts that will arise from this isolated identity will not lead us toward yoga. Whenever we believe these thoughts, we will find ourselves in a state of conflict, for this knowledge has nothing to do with reality. It is totally imagined by the individual within their field of consciousness, it's a self-created delusion. Yet through the practice of yoga one may learn and begin to transcend them. As pramanna increases so the correct knowledge increases within oneself, then one is naturally able to shine the light of pramanna and the corrective intellect burns away these vrittis, this incorrect knowledge.

शब्दज्ञानानुपाती वस्तुशून्यो विकल्पः ॥ ९ ॥

1:9 Shabdajnaananupati vastu shoonyo vikalpah

Both sutras 8 and 9 are similar in that they both discuss creating limitation. It is important for us to realize that the perceiver perceives from their state of consciousness. Wrong knowledge can also have the backing of observation but because one has this avidya deep within oneself, one will perceive incorrectly and that very act of perception will confirm the perceiver's point of view. Hence, we find people can be arguing about something which is very obviously wrong yet they perceive it to be absolutely right. We can see that in the fanatics of our world, human beings who are stuck in fanatical ideologies, clinging to something which is obviously incorrect and does not have any backing of reasoning, yet they cling to it with all their might and force. For them it has become a truth.

Vikalpah means incorrect on a conceptual level. There are a lot of words floating around within the thought waves which get a lot of use. But for the user who has no experience of the word, it's purely on the conceptual level. Language is one of the most phenomenal developments of consciousness. It has been of incredible help to humanity. It has enabled our species to grow and evolve, to exchange ideas and knowledge. Yet we can find that it can also be an extremely limiting factor for a lot of human beings, who merely remain in the realm of words without ever really experiencing what the word is trying to convey. For example, with the word god or the word love or the word gratefulness, one might just stay on the level of the conceptual meaning and never go to the depth of what that word is actually trying to convey. This kind of conceptual content, words just floating on this level, lacking any actual visceral knowledge, is also a klishta, a mental activity which creates interference. Yet when refined this same capacity for language can help us, so it is only limiting when it is backed by incorrect knowledge.

Another meaning of vikalpah is imagination and imagination is of incredible value to us when used in the correct manner, for it can help us to transcend wherever we are. For example, one might approach the concept, 'I am totality', Aham Brahmasmi. Now if one just holds onto this as a word and says, "Oh, I know who I am, I'm totality," this can be a delusion, for this is not correct knowledge. It is only the idea of knowledge, only a faint glow of knowledge. Even though this statement is true, "I am totality," when this statement is not backed by contemplation, meditation and the accompanying experience that follows that, then it becomes useless. However, when we are using our imagination in the correct manner, it is a technique for us to gain true knowledge. Once we have refined our consciousness, then our capacity for imagination is of incredible value to us.

Patanjali is warning us against getting stuck in knowledge merely on the conceptual level, knowledge only on the level of the word. Instead, he is inviting us to use our faculty of imagination, to use our faculty of Brahmana, to go deeper into the experience of the meaning. The word is like the tip of the iceberg, we must dive down deep into the depths because then the knowledge is no longer an obstacle, then it becomes a supporter of the experience and practice of yoga, of unity.

अभावप्रत्ययालम्बना वृत्तिर्निद्रा ॥ १० ॥

1:10 Abhavapratyayalambana vrittir nidra

In the previous sutra, Patanjali has been talking about experiences within the content of consciousness. In this sutra, he discusses sleep, that even sleep is an event in the field of consciousness. It is a thought wave, a thought wave of nothingness and can be verified when we study the human physiology. What we call sleep is actually an experience taking place within a certain area of the brain while the body stays awake. The lungs, the liver, the pancreas and so on, do not sleep. The bio-mechanisms throughout the body continue to maintain their function even though the individual is experiencing sleep, which is distinct from dreaming. For in dreams there is content floating within one's consciousness, so there is a clear distinction between dreaming and deep sleep. In the state of deep sleep, devoid of any dream, we find what Patanjali calls an event in the field of consciousness. Even at that level, we find that the whole brain does not sleep, the whole brain actually never sleeps within an individual's lifetime. The whole the nervous system never sleeps, only a certain part within the nervous system rests during the experience of sleep. Sleep is an experience within the field of consciousness and consciousness never sleeps. That is why when one wakes up, one is aware that one was asleep.

Sometimes in the beginning of our meditation, as we experience the awareness starting to move toward the direction of deep stillness, we find that sleep starts to happen, the experience of sleep starts to arise. This is because we have only experienced that level of stillness, that level of silence, that level of nothingness, when we have been in deep sleep and so are unable to feel a distinction between meditativeness and sleep. Through practice, consistent practice, our awareness can reach that level of silence which is beyond sleep.

अनुभूतविषयासंप्रमोषः स्मृतिः ॥ ११ ॥

1:11 *Anubhoota vishayasanpramoshah smritih*

Here Patanjali explains that even memory is a modification of consciousness. Smriti is memory, that which is once experienced and not forgotten. For one to remember anything there has to be the experience of it first. So memory follows experience, experience precedes memory. Patanjali describes memory as those vrittis, those modifications, that arise within the field of consciousness and which are not forgotten, that do not get stolen, that do not dissolve. They start to become the memory within the individual, then this memory recycles itself over and over again. We find that this memory can be conscious and it can be unconscious, for all memory is ultimately arising from certain vritti, certain unresolved experiences. All memory arises from experience and these experiences can be internal or external.

Memory is also of value to us as our higher experiences will remain in our memory too, thus making our mental activity favorable. When we have experiences not of yoga, but of pain and trauma, we find that that content, that memory, is in our consciousness. But as we continue to practice and experience greater values of self, we have greater experiences within ourself and these experiences will also start to log into our memory, so they will then have a greater recall value. Any individual who has accumulated greater experiences within their own consciousness will know that when these experiences arise they are of great value; they give one a great sense of bliss. For example, you might have a great experience of profound love, a unity experience, an experience of grace, and it has a great recall value. At any moment, you can initiate it in the field of your mind and that experience, that memory, can shift the way you are experiencing that very moment. So even the memory has klishtaklishtah, both natures, to it. It can be interfering and it can be supporting. When we face the memories of our conditioning, which are limiting, we have to clear them. Through our practice, we correct our intellect and create a new memory base to such a level that even when the body drops and we start to experience unity, the memory of that unity remains, the memory of samadhi remains. Then when we are reborn, we already have the imprint of samadhi etched into our consciousness.

अभ्यासवैराग्याभ्यां तन्निरोधः ॥ १२ ॥

1:12 Abhyasa vairagyabhyan tannirodhah

Abhyasa, continued practice. Vairagyabhyan, the birth of detachment. Tannirodhah, ceases. Through the continued practice, Patanjali says, detachment happens. Vairagyabhyan. the birth of a transcendental state of consciousness, where attachment falls away. People often misunderstand this sutra and think he's saying through the practice of detachment, the fluctuations of the mind that he has previously discussed in the Yoga Sutras, are stopped. This is not what Patanjali is saying at all. He is saying that through the practice, not of detachment, but through the continued practice of yoga in its truest sense, not in the reductionist sense as merely trying to get your foot behind your head, but through the practice, the state and the experience of yoga, then naturally what starts to happen is vairagyam. What is vairagyam? Non-identification. And with that comes detachment.

Mind you, detachment is not the opposite of attachment. The English language sometimes has its limitations in translating Sanskrit. It often lacks the depth. When Patanjali says vairagyam, he's not just speaking of detachment as an opposite state to attachment, but detachment as a transcendental state. A transcendental awareness to attachment. Attachment is a state which is dense, which is confused. When the being is dominated by the ego identity, they are in a state of attachment. Whoever they encounter they get attached to, then they project onto it and want to own it. That leads to suffering. Attached to the conditioned belief system, attached to its limited point of view, attached to its relationships. This attachment is not love. This attachment is bondage. This attachment is suffering. This attachment is projection. This attachment is a state of weakness, a state of stress, a state of fear.

Vairagyam, however, is a state that naturally starts to happen as you go through your practice, go deeper and deeper into the state of yoga. Your consciousness starts to expand and natural self-observation begins to occur. In this natural self-observation, you find yourself becoming free of all the attachments that you have been holding onto. You find yourself in a state of spaciousness, where all that you have been tightly holding onto, all that has been consuming you, starts to naturally fall away. You start to see your attachments. You start to see the obsessive behavior. You start to see the obsessive thought patterns and there is a distance between you and what is occurring here. There is a natural witness consciousness that starts to get stronger in you. There is a sense of impersonal awareness that starts to develop between you and you. That is the beauty of it, you see. You are then able to witness yourself from an impersonal state that has no judgement. You are able to see this limited identity getting attached, being afraid, being consumed by the fear of loss and the behavior being dominated by fear. This is the limited identity waiting for Godot, waiting for that moment to arrive when it can live and experience life fully. It is the great paradox of life that everyday that you live, you come closer to death. Yet there is such an attachment to these false ideas and belief systems, this false identity, which keeps us locked into the small cages we have constructed for ourselves, isolated from one another, repeating patterns over and over again that arise from this limited identity.

Patanjali is saying that transformation happens through the continued practice of yoga, not a fluctuating practice mind you, but yoga as a way of life. He is not referring to doing an hour of Hatha flow twice a week. No, he is talking about when you start to experience yoga and be in the state of yoga on a continuous level. Then this continued awareness naturally gives birth to a state in you where your attachments to your false identity will just fall away. You can engage fully with the world, in absolute totality. You are able to engage with all your being and yet you are not enslaved by it. You see, this is an incredible state of freedom. You are able to playfully engage, fully engage, with the manifest world and yet not be consumed by it, because now you have become established more and more in unity consciousness.

Detachment, tannirodhah, Patanjali says, is a natural state. This detachment, this transcendental state, naturally gives rise to a consciousness which is not obsessed with catching hold of all the little fluctuations that happen in life. You are able to be totally aware of these fluctuations of life within the field of your consciousness. They arise, they peak and they disappear. They arise, they peak and they disappear. And when they do, you are able to take the relevant action. Where you need to engage, you engage totally, absolutely. And when you need to surrender, you surrender fully. This is a very powerful state, this state that arises in you when you go deeper and deeper into a transcendental state of consciousness, move more and more toward unity consciousness, toward god consciousness. Naturally, detachment starts to occur in you. You no longer need the attachments, you have less fear, less suffering. You're no longer attached to your rigid point of view. You're no longer attached to the people in your life. That does not mean you don't celebrate them, that you don't care for them, or you don't admire them, but you are no longer viscerally invested in them. Now there is a spaciousness in you, you're no longer projecting your own identity on the things and beings in your life. Instead, you're able to take radical responsibility for your own experience and you're able to give freedom to the people in your life to have their own experience. You no longer play the victim role and create villains. You realize everybody is behaving according to their state of consciousness. If you ask a monkey to clean your room, what do you think a monkey will do? The monkey will be a monkey in your room. You can't complain that the monkey has made a mess in your room, the monkey is behaving like a monkey. But it is the attachment to false expectations, the attachment to the victim identity, which creates all this confusion. The beauty of the practice of yoga is that it naturally brings us to a state of transcendence, where all our false attachments fall away. Our obsession with our limited identity and trying to protect that limited identity, that isolated identity, will naturally fall away. Then what arises is inner freedom.

As you begin to locate this freedom within you, it starts to radiate through you like a warm glow and permeate all dimensions of your life. Now you will find a natural state of freedom in you relationships, a natural state of freedom in your activities that will give you greater and greater access to intelligence, greater and greater access to a more playful and less burdened life. As I have said, attachment leads to burden but detachment, vairagyam, is not the state of apathy. It is the state where your intellect is corrected and so it is able to give full attention to the Is-ness of Is-ness without projecting, without having any false investment. This is a state of great spaciousness. So what Patanjali is saying is that through your continued practice, you naturally start to get established in the state of yoga and one of the great facets of the state of yoga is detachment, vairagyam. You are no longer attached to, or identified with, anything that moves in the relative world. What that means is that you're realizing your true power and you're no longer giving way to the fluctuations of the consciousness. You are keeping the power within the field of consciousness and thereby having a greater capacity to engage, a greater capacity to relate and a greater capacity to experience this great gift of life. Brilliant, isn't it?

तत्र स्थितौ यत्नोऽभ्यासः ॥ १३॥

1:13 Tatra sthitau yatno abhyasah

स तु दीर्घकालनैरन्तर्यसत्कारासेवितो दृढभूमिः ॥ १४॥

1:14 Sa tu dirghakala nairantarya satkara sevito *dridhabhoomih*

In sutras 13 and 14, Patanjali says irrespective of what is going on in the theatre of life, irrespective of what is going on on the relative value, as long as you keep coming back to the practice of yoga, the whole practice: yama, niyama, asana, pranayama, pratyahara, dharana, dhyana, samadhi. Coming back and getting established, going deeper and deeper, then within the practice you will find a natural freedom. You do not let any excuses creep in, because be aware, your mind will come up with all sorts of excuses. The distracted mind will go window-shopping, will come up with doubts, will get forgetful, become consumed by either too much craving or too many aversions. It will be consumed by these distractions so you have to be alert, be aware of this movement of the mind, and then return to the practice in whichever way you can.

As you cultivate your uninterrupted, continuous practice, you will then begin to discover that an interruption starts to occur not on the level of your practice, but on the level of your behavioral patterns, it will start to interrupt the flow of your conditioned life. You can experience this right now. If you are experiencing any kind of toxicity in your mind, any kind of victimhood on the level of your identity, then practice the whole of yoga, right now, in this very moment. Come to a state of absolute stillness within yourself. If you pay attention to the witness within you, you will find that the behavioral pattern has been interrupted, the persistent thought that was repeating itself has been interrupted. A great silence will envelope you and you will find a great sense of power arises in you. You will be able to see that you are expanding and as you expand, your consciousness will fill the room and then go beyond the room and fill the whole planet, then fill the whole solar system. Then your consciousness will fill the whole intergalactic universe and whatever problem you think you have will become very insignificant. As it becomes insignificant, it will loosen its grip over you and become replaced by a deep sense of gratefulness. Not a gratefulness that is for something or someone, not a gratefulness which is based on a weak identity, but a gratefulness which is the essential nature of realization. Try it. The pattern can be interrupted right now.

As the practice of yoga becomes established in your routine, as the being falls in love with the practice, then the practice becomes your way of life and the individual starts to find a natural evolution. When the practice has become firmly established, embedded, on the level of I am-ness, then no amount of fluctuation that occurs in the relative world can shake you. Do you realize how incredibly powerful that state is? That is the state of invincibility. There is no resistance anymore. You start to be in a state of absolute non-resistance and the Being who has reached the state of non-resistance is invincible. That Being cannot be destroyed. When you become non-resistant to the Is-ness of Is-ness that does not mean you don't have your preferences. Of course, you have your preferences, you have your sense of individuality, but within those preferences is also this deep capacity to be non-resistant to whatever is arising. Invincibility, you are indestructible, no one can destroy you, that is the state of yoga. That only occurs as you go deeper and deeper and become established in the practice of yoga, in the state of yoga, and it happens now.

दृष्टानुश्रविकविषयवितृष्णस्य
वशीकारसंज्ञा वैराग्यम् ॥ १५॥

1:15 **Drishtanushravika vishaya vitrishnnasy
vashikara samjna vairagyam**

Patanjali is talking about the state and the practice
of vairagyam, detachment, which is a fundamental
value for the practice, the state and the experience
of yoga. When the state of consciousness which is
established in vairagyam is reached, there is a
natural release from the craving for the sensory
objects, objects we appreciate through our senses
that one has experienced, as well as the sensory
objects that one has not yet experienced. Now, this
can be very easily misunderstood as some
puritanical teaching, but it is anything but that.
What Patanjali is saying is that when we establish
ourselves in the state of vairagyam, we become
more and more innocent, in that there is no
holding onto any experience, there is no addictive
pattern remaining within us. This natural state
arises where there is no longer craving or
aversion. In the lower mind desire is experienced
as a disturbance. When desire arises in the lower
mind, which is not yet established in the state of
vairagyam, then that desire arises as a disturbance
and once the desire is experienced, it often leaves
a trace behind. If a desire accompanies the
experience of great pleasure, it can leave a trace
that can then create a sense of missing, a longing
for that experience to be had again. Or sometimes,

we find that it can lead to a sense of shame or guilt. The human relationship to desire is complex in the lower mind. So naturally, as we start to expand our consciousness and we start to make contact with the true nature of Self, there is this natural letting go of craving and aversion.

In the beginning stages of vairagyam, one finds that the tendency of attachment is very much there. One has to consciously practice and consciously be aware of this tendency of holding on, of converting this process so that pleasure turns into pain through one's attachment to it. So the yogi, the sadhaka, will find that there is a struggle, a tendency toward a restless mind wanting, holding on, craving. It is not the desire which is at fault, it is the experience of desire. In the lower mind conflict is created, but as one evolves, one finds a certain level of mastery where one can consciously, mindfully, choose wholesome actions, wholesome thoughts, wholesome desires. Then to a greater degree, one is able to transcend and let go of unwholesome actions, unwholesome behavior and unwholesome thoughts. However, traces of the old tendencies of attachment can still linger, traces of identification, of converting pleasure into pain. The lower mind constantly engages in that behavior. It turns its gifts into its own weapons and then those gifts become the obstacle.

A lot of the time, people are able to let go of the sensory object, sensory desire, simply because they don't have the capacity to achieve it. That is not a true form of vairagyam, letting go just because they don't have the capacity to access it. That is more a kind of giving up. It is not actually letting go, it is not the supreme state of vairagyam. Vairagyam is not a pessimistic approach to life. It is a quality, a high state of consciousness, it is not giving up on life. The natural increase in your ability has to be accompanied by a state of vairagyam; that is what makes us more and more successful in life. The more we hold on to, the more we are attached to, the more we are fighting the natural flow of life. The yogi, through the practice of vairagyam, starts to become free of the lower tendencies of the mind, from desire being a disturbing value. To the mind established in yoga, established in vairagyam, desire is no longer disturbing. In a higher state of consciousness, the supreme vairagyam is filled with bliss. The lower mind's struggle between this duality of craving and aversion, pleasure and guilt, is no longer present anymore and instead it is filled with ecstasy. In this state, pleasure is no longer the opposite of pain, the pleasure and pain-wrestling duel is no longer there.

It is very important that we enjoy life. That is of paramount importance. We must enjoy life otherwise what is the point of it? This whole idea of life as something that is not to be enjoyed is a very outdated, pessimistic idea that really has no relevance today. Actually it never did have any relevance. So once the yogi is in the state of supreme bliss, the ability to not get held back by any obsessive thoughts or patterns naturally occurs. One must be aware that in the beginning of one's evolutionary journey, one has to release unwholesome desires, unwholesome habits and patterns that are karmic. Discipline and self-regulation are of paramount importance. If the self-regulation is not there, then one is enslaved by the lower mind. Once that self-regulation is mastered and one becomes established, then naturally vairagyam is there. At that point, one rises above the constant craving and aversion and one's relationship to pleasure is devoid of pain. In a higher state of vairagyam, the lower struggle of the mind is no longer there. The desire naturally arises and is experienced. This desire which arises in a consciousness established in vairagyam is a desire which now has the backing of nature; it is natural desire and this desire is designed to be fulfilled. This desire then helps evolve the individual. When the yogi can observe the unfulfilled desire in the lower mind, hiding in the subconscious and giving rise to tension and frustration, they can use this hidden energy to propel themselves into growth and evolution.

What is unfulfilled desire? If you really, rationally observe it, there is nothing called unfulfilled desire. The only thing is an unfulfilled human being. As long as that unfulfillment remains there will be unfulfilled desire, because even if the desire is fulfilled, the unfulfilled human being will, within time, return to their unfulfilled nature. In the unfulfilled human being, there is an endless state of something missing and this state creates greater and greater stress, aggression and confusion. So as the yogi reaches the state of fulfilment, the desires are no longer unfulfilled. For if the yogi is fulfilled, only fulfilling desires can arise.

As the yogi gets established in the practice of vairagyam, they know when they have a desire whether it is a time to act on it, or if it is a time to let go of it, for they have already gone through the stage of being aware of the wholesome and unwholesome desires. This wholesome and unwholesome is not a puritanical state. When one says wholesome and unwholesome desire, it means a desire which helps one grow and expand, it is not a puritanical idea. One first observes within oneself whether this action, this desire, is going to expand oneself and not be destructive to oneself or to others. These desires have the backing of the state of vairagyam, this deep state of inner fulfilment, of recognition, of not holding on, this inner self-regulation. Then, more and more bliss arises and life is experienced with greater joy. You enjoy life, which is very important.

तत्परं पुरुषख्यातेर्गुणवैतृष्ण्यम् ॥ १६ ॥

1:16 Tat paran purusha khyate gunavaitrishnyam

Here, Patanjali builds upon the subject of detachment. The highest moment of detachment is realized when the being is starting to see their own essential nature and their false identity just falls away. What if, in this very moment, you could see the infinity of who you are? Would you still hold on so tight? Would you not feel a sense of ease within your heart, feel the grip loosen? Would you not realize the absurdity of this fear of loss? Because you can experience it in this moment, you can see your essential nature in this very moment, the infinity of who you are. You can witness your essential nature but you will have to correct your intellect, you will have to correct your mind. As I said in sutra 3, tada drastuh svarupe avasthanam, the seer's perception corrects itself. You will have to correct your individuality and align it with this realization. Integration, by which I mean this awareness, happens in time but the transcendence happens now. The transcendence can occur now but the integration happens more slowly, over time, as you maintain a consistency in your practice and your life has a greater and greater value of yoga. You deepen now and as you deepen into that awareness of pure consciousness, through your practice you will start to transcend. You begin to transcend the grosser laws of nature, of birth and death, the grosser laws of nature that dominate this body. For within this body is the great Being who is beyond the laws of nature, beyond the fluctuations and you can see that now. As you see your essential Self, the big S, it dawns in your awareness and starts to glow, to radiate through you, the celestial glow of Self. Then you will find you loosen your grip on the false identity and the fear will leave you. That happens now, through the practice of yoga and continues happening now. As you become more and more established in the state of detachment, not holding on too tight to anything or anyone, this spaciousness arises, this great sense of play arises. You become the great explorer of life, you become the great taster of the gifts of life. You are no longer afraid or in conflict with this great gift of life.

वितर्कविचारानन्दास्मितारूपानुगमात् संप्रज्ञातः ॥ १७॥

1:17 Vitarkavicharanandasmitaroopanugamat samprajnatah

In sutra 16, Patanjali talks about the great bliss from detachment, vairagyam, that arises and here in sutra 17, he discusses the different aspects of samadhi, unity experience. Samprajnata, sam is totality, unity, wholeness and prajna means awareness. So here he is talking about an experience of wholeness in one's awareness.

Of course, there are multiple meanings to this sutra. One is that as this unity experience starts to occur it has four stages or levels: vitarka, vichara, ananda and asmita. Through the practice, when we go deeper into ourself, this fluid awareness starts to occur. One can perceive within oneself the sense of I am-ness, independent of all else. On the surface level is vitarka, meaning correct reasoning. Beneath that is vichara, clear perception, clear observation. Then ananda, inner bliss and then asmita is experienced, I am-ness, the pure field of I am-ness; so within the experiences of I am-ness is the experience of bliss as I am. Within that bliss arises clear perception and that clear perception gives rise to clear knowledge. It can be perceived in a different way as well, that as we are going deep within ourself, we transcend reasoning and our analytical mind, we transcend all knowledge, we transcend all external perception, vichara, and we start to take that perception inward. This is a very special kind of perception, where instead of it being object-focused, the subject is using the object to ultimately realize that the object does not exist independently of its own value. All objects are merely a reflection of what is contained within the field of consciousness of the subject who is witnessing it. As we go deeper into that, there arises an inner bliss and that inner bliss gives rise to the accompanied experience of I am-ness, the infinite value of I am-ness. As one goes into the state of samprajnata samadhi, that fluid state where the I am-ness is maintained, I am the infinite, there is an awareness of inner bliss giving rise to inner cognition, clear cognition, which gives birth to correct intellect, an intellect which corrects itself. In the yogic teachings there is a sutra which says that through the experience of samadhi, samadhi is experienced, that within the experience of samadhi are all the answers, within the experience of samadhi everything gets resolved. Samadhi resolves everything. So samadhi, in Sanskrit, is also used as a word for resolution.

As the experience of unity starts to dawn within us, we find an inner resolution arises. As this inner resolution is experienced, it is accompanied by the experience of I am-ness, the true value of Self that gives birth to cognition of inner bliss, ananda, which gives birth to clear cognition, vichara, clear thought. If one goes in the direction of thought, one will find that the thought is clear, but first, one must transcend thought in order to access the inner bliss. If one is only on the level of thought and analysis, then one cannot experience the inner bliss. For one cannot experience inner bliss by thinking about bliss. In the experience of bliss is the transcendence of all thoughts of bliss, one is just in the experience of bliss. When one has spent enough time in the experience of bliss, only then can one move one's awareness in the direction of thought. Eventually those thoughts will start to have the value of bliss. Then one's perception will start to have the value of bliss. But if one remains purely on the level of analysis and thought, then one cannot have access to ananda and asmita. Samprajnata is that state of fluid awareness where all four stages are maintained. We start to refine our capacity to be attentive in our meditation, so that we can then take any object in our meditation and that object will start to reveal its secrets to us.

Here, Patanjali is giving us a tool to access great knowledge, correct knowledge, knowledge which is beyond the physical realm. We start to have knowledge of the unmanifest level of reality, the level that is beyond the physical realm, that is the experience of bliss. I am-ness, I am bliss, without any object, without any knowledge, beyond all that and even subtler still, the great field of silence. One can verify it within one's own practice as one goes deeper. All this can be experienced in one fluid stroke, the bliss is within the I am-ness where the I am-ness is maintained. As one moves one's awareness in the direction of thoughts, one sees that thoughts are resolved, which gives you clear insight into what you must do next. You find that a clear, resolved answer starts to arise. But if we are stuck on the level of reasoning, thinking, analyzing and perceiving, we are not going into the level of ananda and asmita. Then vichara becomes limiting within our own practice. So this thinking and analyzing has to be transcended, accepted and integrated within the experience.

This fluid state is a very desirable state to experience, where you are gaining awareness of the external realm in its fullest value and the external realm starts to reveal its secrets, the corresponding cosmic value. The inner experience of I am-ness and bliss are maintained and this lamp of awareness starts to burn. Both the inner awareness is fluid and the external awareness is fluid. One's thoughts are clear; clear thinking and clear perception accompany the experience of inner bliss and I am-ness. But when one goes into the practice, one finds that one first confronts one's reasoning, analytical mind and one needs to transcend that to achieve ananda and asmita, the I am-ness. So samprajnata is that state of unity, fluid unity, and samyama is where the four aspects, vitarka, vichara, ananda and asmita, bind together to create a tool for deeper knowledge and the state of fluid awareness, I am-ness, I am infinity, I am bliss.

विरामप्रत्ययाभ्यासपूर्वः संस्कारशेषोऽन्यः ॥ १८॥

1:18 Virama pratyayabhyasa poorvah samskarashesho anyah

Through the consistent practice and maintenance of this state of bliss, another state naturally begins to arise in oneself where all samskara burns away. There are two meanings to this sutra. One is that through the consistent practice and maintenance of this state of samprajnata samadhi, all samskara start to burn away. All conditioning which is limiting starts to be burned away; all incorrect knowledge, incorrect cognition, starts to be burned away. Then through the awareness, one starts to move in the direction of the subtler dimension of reality. One finds, through one's practice, the experience starts to arrive through the maintaining of samprajnata samadhi, that is, you transcend all impressions and all movement and there is a total experience of non-local self, a totally cosmic experience, even the I am-ness drops. This samadhi is asamprajnata or nirvichara, when there is no mind, no object, only infinite peace, infinite Being, the light of god, dominates. One feels bigger than the universe. This state comes and goes within one's practice, it is not constantly available. Samprajnata can be constantly available, that I am-ness, the pure awareness witnessing and giving birth to bliss with clear perception of thought, clear intellect, but the asamprajnata samadhi comes and goes, the experience comes and goes. Samprajnata (also known as savikalpa) and asamprajnata (also known as nirvikalpa) are directly related to each other, united with one another; neither one is a lower or higher state. When samprajnata is maintained consistently, it gives birth to asamprajnata, coming and going. This coming and going of asamprajnata refines the samprajnata experience. As the awareness expands inward in the direction of silence, then this experience naturally becomes much more capable in the dynamic field of reality.

In the practice of our yoga, we find in the asamprajnata experience that there is a pure experience of oneness, no mind, no thought, no isolated self, just pure experience of unity. All activity has ceased. All samskaras start to be burned, good and bad ones. It goes beyond all duality to the experience of the pure non-dual Self. As one moves between samprajnata and asamprajnata, one ultimately starts to access what is called a sahaj samadhi and the effortless state is maintained. The cosmic value maintains itself along with one's daily activity, but one finds that one is not distracted in one's daily activity from the inner awareness of wholeness. Ultimately, this is what we want to cultivate within ourself, this state of sumyama, fluid awareness, where the awareness of the inner cosmic world is maintained while one is playing a role to its fullest value in the relative field of reality. The yogi favors this. We are not against the relative field of reality. We are interested in experiencing it in all its fullness, while still experiencing the absolute field within oneself in all its fullness too. Samprajnata and asamprajnata, together, simultaneously, giving birth in their unity to sahaj, the effortless state of unity, greater and greater unity.

भवप्रत्ययो विदेहप्रकृतिलयानाम् ॥ १९॥

1:19 Bhavapratyayo videha prakritilayanam

If we maintain these states of consciousness that Patanjali has been discussing, then even when the body drops, even when one is in astral form, this awareness maintains itself. When one is born again in this physical form, the memory of this unity consciousness remains; the memory of samadhi remains and this, of course, helps one to evolve further. Maintaining this state becomes a meditative experience, the unity continues and this punya, this virtue, helps one in one's journey onward, whether in this realm or in others.

श्रद्धावीर्यस्मृतिसमाधिप्रज्ञापूर्वक
इतरेषाम् ॥ २० ॥

1:20 Shraddha virya smriti samadhiprajna poorvaka itaresham

Patanjali describes the five qualities we must cultivate within our consciousness to help support our realization of the state of yoga. He is a very smart guy. He is aware of the obstacles that will arise, the tendencies we humans have to find ways to distract ourselves from our path. He is under no illusion and he is not claiming that the journey will be effortless. He does not take a stand either way, he doesn't say the journey is difficult or easy. Instead, he guides us in a way which is supportive to the practice, to the state of yoga and to our realization. The five qualities that Patanjali says are immensely helpful to the yogi are sraddha, virya, smriti, samadhi and prajna. If we cultivate these within our consciousness, within our own inner state, then these five qualities will support us on our journey. The law of nature is that whatever you give attention to will grow. So when we give our attention to these five qualities within our own being, they will start to get stronger. We will start to develop the muscles within our own consciousness on both the level of thought and a subtler level as well.

The first quality Patanjali refers to is sraddha, trust. Sraddha has a deep meaning here, it does not mean believe as it is sometimes translated. Here, the first meaning that arises from sraddha is the state, the practice and the experience of trust. Trust is one of the first expressions of love, but the trust that Patanjali is talking about is not in somebody else, that trust is nothing more than a controlling mechanism of the ego. When the ego says, "I trust you" to someone, it has a particular idea of how that person must behave and then when they don't behave within that parameter, the ego says, "Ah, my trust was broken." This is not the trust that Patanjali is talking about here. The sraddha that we are interested in is of an unbreakable quality. This trust is not in some alien entity sitting on a distant white, fluffy cloud. The sraddha here, the trust, is the recognition of love. It is the first quality we must cultivate; this attitude, this deep recognition of the eternal truth that is loving us. Patanjali does not mean blind faith. It is not a dogmatic belief. This is trust which arises from a corrected intellect. As you correct your intellect, you really start to understand that it is love that is guiding you. But if your lower intellect has not yet been corrected, then it will have a tendency to drive you toward fear, toward doubt and uncertainty. It seems to be a chronic issue of humanity. So you have to overcome these tendencies of your lower intellect, your ego, and you need to feed that level of your intellect which has the correct knowledge. So here, trust is actually recognizing the truth and that recognition then gets you into a state of receptivity. You develop a trust in your practice, a trust in the infinite organizing power of nature. Trust ultimately in trust. And when we speak of trust in the infinite organizing power of nature, again, we are not talking about some alien entity. The organizing power of nature is you. You are That.

The cultivation of this practice of sraddha helps us move the way love makes us move. In the absence of this trust, this ability to surrender to the great intelligence, our actions and behaviors are dominated by fear. We move the way fear makes us move. Love and fear cannot coexist in the same bucket. Either you are in love or you are in fear. That does not mean that when you are experiencing love that fear might not arise. The fear might well still arise, but now it is not the dominating factor in your consciousness. You are not suppressing it either. You are holding it in the light of your awareness, the awareness that knows that any action, whether on the level of thought or on a physical level, is guided from this deep acknowledgement of the flow of love. The love is always loving you, right now, wherever you are and that is a fact. For are you not effortlessly here? The heart is beating, the cells are communicating with each other, trillions of cells are talking to each other effortlessly, without you really having to do anything. There is a great intelligence floating in you, that very same intelligence that has become the sun, the moon, the stars, the entire intergalactic universe, and right now it is expressing itself as you. Now, be with that for a while. This is not some esoteric, mythical idea. This is your very visceral experience. As you be with that, you will realize that what arises there is love. Let go of the fear and let in the love. Fear is merely the bluff of the mind, based on a lie which has been told so many times that it feels like it is truth. That is the nature of lies. If you keep saying something over and over again, then, to the conditioned mind, it starts to become a truth.

The first quality, Patanjali says, that the yogi needs to cultivate, is a deep trust, that radical quality of trust, for trust is one of the finest expressions of love, sraddha, trust, reverence, surrender. Surrendering to the cosmic intelligence that is you. Right now, you are the ears, the mouth, the eyes of the whole cosmos. The totality of the cosmos is experiencing itself through your nervous system. As you realize that, there is a natural reverence that arises and that gets you in a state of receptivity. Here trust helps you act in alignment with the evolutionary intelligence and at the same time, it helps you receive what arises in this moment. Trust serves the dual purpose of acting in alignment with the natural intelligence, with the force of love instead of the illusionary force of fear. It allows you to get into a state of receptivity, so you can receive the great abundance of nature. In all traditions, the ultimate state has been described as love. If there is a god, the nature of that god has to be love, not judgment. Judgement only exists in the absence of love. Judgement of itself and of others is a clear symptom of the absence of love.

Virya, passion, is the second quality that Patanjali invokes, passion and energy. Vir in Sanskrit means the warrior, not the warrior in the context of violence, somebody who is going to get stuck in their reactionary tendencies. Here virya is referring to the quality of immense courage, from which the natural outcome is trust. So virya means an intensity of passion where the yogi is filled with passion for the practice and for life as practice. This passion and energy naturally arises when there is sraddha, when one surrenders to the guiding love within and releases all effort to control it. When you are really showing up to the practice with a deep faith, a deep trust, a deep reverence, not only in your sadhana but in your whole life, then as you begin to cultivate this sraddha you will find that your life becomes your practice and you are naturally filled with strength and an intense energy. That is virya.

Sometimes when you are meditating, the meditation is filled with an immense silence and sometimes the meditation is filled with thought, but you can never have a bad meditation. That's just an illogical idea created by the mind. As I always say, if you jump in the water you will get wet. When you're not judging the experience, that is your meditation, that is your practice. When you are not trying to control it and you have trust, then virya occurs. Then you will start to cultivate this energy, this passion, this quality of intensity.

There are many practices and techniques in yoga to help support the energy system of the body, unlike the so-called energy drinks and boosters that recreate certain biochemicals to manufacture a false sense of energy. This is much subtler than that. Virya is an intensity that fills you with the optimal levels of energy. In our contemporary culture there seems to be a crisis of energy. Human beings don't seem to have optimal levels of energy and need all kinds of energy drinks to function throughout the day. Stress is a common factor in our work places. People struggle to have just enough energy to live and therefore all sorts of addictive behaviors are increasing. That is why, in the tantric practices, there is immense focus on cultivating a strong, energetic body. We must cultivate an energy-rich environment within our own physiology, within our own energetic body and within our consciousness. An environment which is energy-rich, not energy-depleted, can then produce any powerful action. The surrender which arises from an energy-depleted environment is not true surrender, it is just giving up. The true surrender can only arise from an energy-rich environment. That surrender has value. So a yogi must cultivate an energy-rich environment. That is why we must practice the techniques that not only build our physical strength, but sharpen our intellect and build our energetic strength, too.

Patanjali is encouraging us to fill ourselves with this energy and approach the practice as we approach our life, filled with passion, a total commitment with no half-assing. Wherever you are in life, be fully present to everything in any moment, then you will find you have access to infinite energy. Through your practice, through the techniques of yoga, the subtler practices of yoga, the kriyas and the prana practices, you will start to develop an energy-rich environment within your body and then beyond. As you develop this energy-rich environment within your being, you start to have access to an energy-rich environment beyond your physiology. That helps to take the practice way beyond that little yoga mat. From that expansion arises courage, realization of invincibility. Mind you, this invincibility is not arrogance; this invincibility is a very deep, subtle realization where you have already experienced a certain level of truth, sraddha virya. Just as you know that the sun is behind the clouds and are no longer fooled by the clouds floating in front of it, then so too, as you develop radical trust, total surrender to the infinite intelligence, you will now understand it and know it on a deeper level. With that knowledge comes a great power, virya, this sense of invincibility, indestructibility, because you realize the essence of you can never be destroyed no matter what somebody projects upon you. No one can control you, no one can have power over your experience, no matter who they are, what position they hold, or what title they have. Virya means courageousness, energy-rich passion, aliveness. This is the quality we must cultivate and through the practice and the experience of yoga, this quality will become more and more available to us.

This intense, optimal energy, this virya, is not a restless energy, it is not hyperactivity. A restless energy is actually not enough energy and its foundation is exhaustion. Patanjali is talking about a balanced, integrated energetic field. A lot of people practice only as a means to an end, to fix a feeling or achieve just enough happiness in their life to get by. But here Patanjali is talking to yogis who are really interested in freedom, who are not interested in mediocrity, but to those who are interested in living and realizing the true greatness within their own consciousness. Mind you, he is not being judgmental to those who are okay with living a mediocre life. He's absolutely indifferent to that. What he is really interested in though, are those who want to experience the true potential of Being. Now, not somewhere in a distant, isolated future, after the body ends and you die and follow a light to the end of a tunnel that leads you finally to some heavenly land. We are here and we are talking about experiencing freedom here, Now, not in the afterlife, but in this life and in this body. Yes, in this body, the body is included. So there is a need to cultivate virya, this intense, optimal energy Now. We have the practices and techniques to do so.

The third quality Patanjali discusses is smriti meaning continued awareness. The nature of the lower mind is to be forgetful, so here Patanjali is talking about the capacity of our higher mind to have a sense of continued awareness. Smriti can sometimes be referred to as mindful, even though it is quite a strange word, mindful, to be mindful. But these days it seems to be used a great deal. So smriti means being aware, being in a state of remembrance, in the context of your personal practice, in your life as a practice, being really clear in your intention, and the purpose of your practice. You have to be mindful because often the ego will hijack your practice, hijack your life. Then it will become about something that is totally different and not your intention at all, because of the conditioning.

Our human nervous system is prone to forgetfulness, it can forget the truth and quickly get lost in the lies. We've all had that experience in our own lives, everyone has had that Ah ha! moment, a glimpse of something you know is good, something that will change your life and help you to embody it. Then life catches up and you lose it. The perspective is gone, a perversion of your values starts to happen. You feel defeated, you feel again burdened by the nitty-gritty of life. You lose your perspective, lose sight of the fact that you are actually floating around in infinite space on a tiny blue dot. A phone call or a message can really shake you up. A little thought, a little speech from somebody saying something negative about you, can turn it all upside down. This is not the quality which Patanjali is supporting. What he is calling for is smriti, remembrance of the truth, keeping your eyes focused on your awareness, holding the value of truth. Then, even when the fluctuating values start to dominate your field of consciousness, you can really hold on to the value which does not fluctuate, the value of truth, the value of yoga, where you and That are ultimately one. Then the perversion of that value cannot hijack your consciousness.

For this pattern of behavior to be interrupted, we must cultivate the quality of smriti, the remembrance of truth, the awareness of truth. Continued awareness is in itself liberating. We must cultivate this quality of alertness, of witness consciousness, being clear of our intention, checking where we are at in our intention. Often, you may find that even though you might have the intention of realizing yourself, the intention of attaining enlightenment, what you will find is your attention is all over the place. As long as your intention and attention are not in alignment, then true realization cannot occur. If intention is the root of the tree, then attention is the trunk. So smriti is the art of uniting your intention and your attention, being alert, cultivating the correct memory, not the memory of your conditioning but the memory of dharma, purposeful living, living intentionally from moment to moment. Often the world will get to you, karma will get to you, life with all its varied distractions will get to you and then the yogi can get swayed and throw away the diamond in exchange for a banana. As my Master used to say to me, don't be a monkey. If you offer a monkey a diamond and a banana, he will throw away the diamond and take the banana, for that is the relevant behavior of a monkey, but not of a human. Here, of course, the diamond is referring to your heart, the quality of your true Self, your true freedom. So the first three qualities Patanjali wants us to cultivate are sraddha, virya, and smriti meaning trust, energy, and continued awareness.

The fourth quality is samadhi. Here samadhi is used in a slightly different context than before. Patanjali is using it in the context of absorption. The yogi has to cultivate absorption within their practice to reach a level of unity with the practice, where ultimately you are no longer practicing. The practice falls away and is just part of you; it is integrated into your very Being. When this integration occurs, it is no longer a practice that is separate from you. You are now living it. It is not a show anymore, not an activity separate from you. It is not a facade that you have built around you to get some kind of validation. When all that drops away, the true practice begins to arise in the very sanctum of your heart. The inner practice of yoga, when you and the practice merge and your practice is not limited to a few poses, trying to get your body into complex positions, when yoga penetrates every aspect of your being, that is Samadhi. Patanjali is also using it in the context of moving toward unity. The yogi should cultivate an awareness that they are moving toward unity, greater and greater unity consciousness, cultivating unity consciousness, practicing unity consciousness, experiencing unity consciousness. At one end of the spectrum is the ego consciousness that is dense, mundane and heavy. Then at the other end is unity consciousness, cosmic consciousness, god consciousness, transcendental; you are awake and moving more and more toward unity consciousness, where you and god are one. At that level of your consciousness, when you reach that level of awareness and there is no separation between you and that, it is no longer just an intellectual idea. It is not only understood on the level of your intellect, it is understood on the level of your visceral experience. So we are absorbing the practice and we are moving toward unity. As we do so, we are cultivating thoughts, we are cultivating visions, and we are correcting our intellect, and continuing to move toward love, toward unity consciousness. That is samadhi.

The fifth quality is prajna. Pra means transcendental, that which is beyond. Sometimes, people reduce prajna to the very limited meaning of should be aware. But here, Patanjali is saying that prajna is the true knowledge which arises from the valid experience of yoga. He is asking us to cultivate this quality of prajna, the quality of knowledge that rises from silence. He is referring to the transcendental knowledge. Now, what does that mean? Prajna is listed here as the fifth quality that the yogi must cultivate and it is the knowledge which arises from silence. As you practice the whole science of yoga: yama, niyama, asana, pranayama, pratyahara, dharana, dhyana, samadhi, meditation and kriya, the whole path of yoga, you start to transcend. So what arises in you now is transcendental knowledge, a transcendental awareness, not just the knowledge that is within the mind, knowledge from your conditioned, linear way of thinking. Now what becomes available to you through your practice is a totally different quality of knowledge, a knowledge which is not burdensome, a knowledge which is not reductionist, a knowledge which is expansive by its nature. The knowledge of the mind, at the level of the mind, is reductionist by its essential nature. It reduces things to concepts and also limits the individual to certain ideas. So prajna is that quality of knowledge which arises when the yogi, through the practice, starts to make contact with the transcendental field, the source of all. A certain level of awareness will start to develop beyond thought, awareness that is a witness. As this witness pays attention, a different kind of movement starts to occur, not movement toward an object but movement within oneself. This movement of consciousness within gives birth to prajna, an intelligence which is not based in thought; it is beyond thought, an intelligence the quality of which is silence. It is beyond the mind, so you are able to observe yourself and as you continue to observe yourself, you will find that this is the key to your evolution, this continuous observation. The observer in you starts to get stronger and that is what we must develop, the observer, the witness. Be a witness to yourself, be a witness to your action, be a witness to your behavior, to the movement that arises in you. You will find that just by merely witnessing yourself that there is a natural self-correction which will start to happen. Most human beings don't have this capacity. They haven't developed this capacity. That's why they are constantly self-sabotaging, constantly acting in ways which are dominated by their subconscious and their unconscious mind. Prajna is the quality of intelligence that starts to become available to you as you start having access to no mind and now, from that place, you can start gaining a certain mastery over the mind.

If you pay attention to all five of these qualities, you will see that they are interconnected. One cannot exist without the other. Sraddha, virya, smriti, samadhi and prajna are all connected. One follows the other, samadhi naturally leads to prajna. As greater unity happens, greater and greater access to non-local knowledge will occur. You will start to have access to knowledge which is beyond your thoughts. You start to gain access to the mind of god, or the universal mind, and it shows up now not as loud thought, but as silence within you. You will start to find that you have a greater silence within and at the same time, a greater intelligence, prajna, that quality of intelligence which is beyond thought. That is the quality of a mind which has been refined. When the individual starts to gain access to that stage, starts to have a certain mastery over the mind, then prajna happens. So you can see the sutra has a double meaning. One, that these five qualities we must cultivate within ourself are in order to deepen our practice and experience in the state of yoga. The other meaning that arises from this sutra is that through the practice of yoga as a whole, the science of evolution, the yogi will start to experience these five qualities fully.

All five of these qualities that Patanjali offers us are a great support to our sadhana and to our life. As we practice and the practice becomes us, these qualities naturally start to arise in our consciousness. They first support us and then, through the practice which is supported, these qualities become available to our consciousness with far less effort. So sraddha, virya, smriti, samadhi and prajna are to be cultivated, experienced and practiced. They will help us to not get stuck and plateau, no matter what state of consciousness we are in. As you bring these qualities into your practice, they will help support you as you continue your journey, so that you don't give up too easily.

तीव्रसंवेगानाम् आसन्नः ॥ २१ ॥

1:21 Tivra sanveganam aasannah

The yogi who cultivates the qualities and the practice of yoga with a sense of intensity and passion has a deep feeling of mumukshutva. In Sanskrit, mumukshutva means a great desire for liberation, for freedom. Those individuals who really cultivate this passion and sanveganam, meaning those who are quick to practice, quick to follow and not procrastinate, have a quality of radiance and are moving toward non-victim identity, have a natural bliss, a natural cheerfulness. They will find themselves to be experiencing yoga sooner, experiencing a greater and greater unity.

Patanjali is not talking about those who just use their practice as an excuse to wait, but to those who are sincerely devoted. Not devoted with a sense of burden, a sense of waiting, but those who are cultivating bliss consciousness, yogic consciousness, sat chit ananda. When these individuals make contact with the teachings, they don't just sit with it, keep it stored in the memory bank. No. When they make contact with the knowledge, they integrate it into their being and then they start to truly practice it. This is a yogi who is moving toward a greater state of consciousness, tivra sanveganam. They have realized that this life is not a waiting room. There seems to be a chronic tendency amongst humanity to treat this life as a waiting room, always waiting for something to arrive, some fantasy idea to happen, procrastinating, getting caught up in the smallness of the mind. Here, Patanjali exalts those who are deeply passionate and have this fire inside, burning to discover, not just to seek, but to discover in greater and greater depth what they have always been seeking. Tivra sanveganam aasannah. For them the state of yoga is very close. The state of unity consciousness becomes closer to those who are deeply passionate and are not giving up, they are cultivating bliss consciousness. These individuals are not victims. They are not practicing from a state of ego. They are achieving a state of yoga. When? Now.

मृदुमध्याधिमात्रत्वात् ततोऽपि

विशेषः ॥ २२॥

1:22 Mridu madhya dhimatratvat tatopi visheshah

Here Patanjali says that the experience of yoga depends on the passion, on the intensity, on the practice of the individual. He is not suggesting you should try to get your body into all kinds of pretzel poses, this is not what he is speaking about here. Patanjali is talking about the intensity of your longing for freedom. Are you using the practice to get somewhere or is the practice itself the destination and the journey? As you truly pour yourself into the practice, then the realization of the state of yoga becomes more and more accessible to you. If the practice is weak, the experience is weak. When the practice is an intense, complete, holistic practice, the experience is holistic. If the practice is imbalanced, lopsided, incomplete, reductionist, then the experience will be that. Mind you, the practice of yoga is designed to let you experience yoga. They are ultimately one, yet on a relative level they are distinct from each other. We must pay attention. It is very important not to get confused. The state of yoga, the practice of yoga and the experience of yoga are three distinct movements.

ईश्वरप्रणिधानाद् वा ॥ २३ ॥

1:23 *Ishvara pranidhanat va*

Ishvara is the name Patanjali has chosen for the manifest Absolute. Ishvara, the Divine, or Ishta, meaning the supreme soul, your higher Self ultimately. Ishvara pranidhanat va. Here he is talking about the deep state of surrender, cultivating the deep state of surrender to the Divine. Mind you, Patanjali's idea of the Divine, of god, is not of some alien being. Ishvara is the very reflection of your Self, the big S, the supreme Self within you and beyond. The cell moving right now in your body, the fire in your heart, the twinkle in your eyes, the skin on your hands, the blood in your wings, the eternal song of your heartbeat, the earth beneath your feet, the whistle of the wind, the sky that envelops you, the intention that arises in you, the seeker and the sought, the discoverer and the discovered, the observer and the observed, this and that, everything and nothing, the finite and the infinite, the light and the shadow, the coming and the going and the one that never comes or goes. There is nothing that is not That. Ishvara pranidhanat va.

Some translators translate this sutra as awe. That by being in awe and devoted to god, you can control your mind. This is not what Patanjali means. What he is talking about here is the cultivation of devotion, the recognition of the Divine within and without is of great service to us in the realization of the state of yoga. But again, he is not talking about devotion as merely an external show or devotion coming from a place of victimhood. Patanjali is talking about the devotion that comes from a deep humility which is moving toward itself. Ishvara pranidhanat va, the state of surrender to the intelligence which is ultimately you. Practicing this total surrender to the Is-ness of Is-ness, this absolute release, this letting go of all desire to control, will help you at any moment in your life, no matter what the anxiety or thought is. If you can release all fear and surrender into trust, you become absolutely non-resistant to what is arising. You lay it all at the feet of totality. Only then will you find yoga in the moment. You will move toward unity because all the fear, all the stress in you, arises when you are moving in the opposite direction to unity, when you're moving toward an ego-dominant consciousness. But, as your individuality begins to move toward unity, as you begin to move toward Ishvara, your higher reflection, the supreme soul, which is ultimately you, then in any moment you will find greater unity, you will find greater bliss, greater joy, greater peace, and therein will arise great power. Ishvara pranidhanat va.

Let go of the fear and let in the Divine, but first refine your understanding of the Divine. The Divine is not sitting behind some barricade in a temple, a church, a synagogue, or a mosque. It is moving as you right now. If there is the omniscient, omnipotent, transcendent Being, then she has to be available right here, right now, in the very fabric of your existence, not in some far off, distant land. You don't need a vehicle to find it or a visa to get to it, you don't need the acknowledgement of the whole world to achieve it. All your problems can exist just the way they are now and you can still experience the Divine. In the very experience of that, all the problems will dissolve. Your perspective will be corrected, your values will be corrected, natural surrender and letting go will happen and you will be filled with a greater sense of divinity within your own heart, Ishvara is within your heart. The kingdom of heaven is within you, right here, within your own heart, right now. The sun, the moon and the stars, the entire intergalactic universe is within your heart. Practice listening to that divine within and as you

listen, you will realize, within and without are just
mere locations from a point of view of the mind.
There is only, Is, Ishvara pranidhanat va.

क्लेशकर्मविपाकाशयैरपरामृष्टः
पुरुषविशेष ईश्वरः ॥ २४॥

1:24 Klesha karma vipaka shayair aparamrishtah
purushavishesh ishvara

Ishvara, which is where Ishta comes from,
meaning the individualized expression of the
infinite. Ishta and Ishvara are one and the same. So
what is Ishta? When you go in the direction of god,
of existence, or what you might also call truth, and
you start to make contact with it, what you will
find is a particular expression of that infinite. It's
the finite expression of the infinite but existing
independently of space-time. That is what
Patanjali is saying here, that Ishvara is that Being,
the individualized expression of that Being, a
special kind of Being independent of time and also
independent of karma. So, no karma and no
conditioning, untouched by past, present, or
future, limitless in its knowledge.

When you have an experience of god, Patanjali
explains, that experience is on a very personal
level, a very personal experience of the infinite. He
says that the most intimate experience of all
experiences is the experience of the infinite within

oneself, the closest experience one has in the context of absolute love. So to talk of the Divine in the context of an impersonal, untouchable god is very unappealing, because ultimately it is one's relationship to oneself. How the infinite rises in our consciousness, how the goddess rises within when one is tuning into a goddess, is a very personal experience. This is Ishta, your personal relationship to the infinite, because the way the Divine will rise and appear in you might not be the same as the goddess that rises in some other person. Your experience of the Divine Mother, or divine feminine, is unique to you, this is Ishta, which Patanjali also calls Ishvara.

When we start to use the techniques of yoga and our consciousness starts to move in the direction of what we call god consciousness, beyond cosmic, what we find is that the Absolute takes the individualized form we have created and so rises in us in an incredibly personal manner. One can verify this from one's own experience. That is why, in the yogic tradition, there are these techniques and practices attached to the particular Ishta. Shiva is an Ishta and Durga is an Ishta, even Kundalini can be an expression of Ishta. So everybody is having an experience that is unique to them and is extremely personal. It is such an intimate experience that it is difficult to explain. You can't really find the words to portray god, the infinite rising within, showing up as a form. Experiencing god defies description because it is the indivisible whole, yet the oneness does not mean sameness. The leaves on the tree are all part of the one tree but no two leaves are the same. Patanjali is saying that Ishvara is the state of awake consciousness, the cosmic god unity.

Ishvara is not bound by one expression. By its very nature it takes on multitudes of expressions. From the tantric prospective, as I have said, the goddess takes on a multitude of forms and is not limited by any of them. Like the colorless sap moving in the direction of the green leaf, it expresses green-ness in that leaf but it is not limited by the green-ness of that leaf. It will move right on into another leaf next to it and that leaf will have its own unique expression of green-ness. They are both made up of the colorless sap so they are ultimately both cosmic; they are the individual expression of the cosmic consciousness. This god experience transcends space and time. So that is why one gets filled with the grace of the Divine. Nobody, in the history of humanity, who has experienced this level of unity consciousness has ever said, "Hey, don't do it. It's not worth it." It's not like when someone comes back from Venice and says, "Yeah, it's ok, but it's overcrowded, it stinks, it's overpriced, it's too touristy." Nobody has gone to this level of consciousness and come down from it and said, "Nah, don't bother. A god experience is really not worth it." You see, this individualized form is seeking to expand its scope of experience. It feels limited when it is encased in this bag of skin, it feels unnatural. When you are having this experience within yourself, you experience the highest potential of Being. You don't really find people who are stuck on the hamster-wheel of life in ecstasy. What you do find are exhausted people suppressing the very act, the very impulse, of creative intelligence. What is the natural impulse of creative intelligence? To expand its scope of experience. So when one starts to go deeper into this state of unity consciousness, one naturally starts to expand. One starts to have the experience of god, not the concept of god. God only as a concept is a useless concept and one better not to have. If one's relationship to god is only on the level of a concept, then it is better to live in a universe where there is no god. The experience of what one calls god is only relevant if one can bring it to one's experience, otherwise it is a very dangerous idea to walk around with.

Yoga is not interested in having a conceptual idea of anything, least of all god. You can start from the concept, but then you must bring it into your experience. The yogis who had these god experiences wrote about it; they wanted to share the teachings with others. Patanjali expresses this experience with such eloquent clarity that you know he can only do this if he has experienced it himself. You can see it in the detail. You can see that what he is discussing is definitely from the viewpoint of the experienced. You can verify this from your own experience. If you practice the right techniques, when you are moving within yourself and you're doing the tantric practice, you find that waves of the infinite are rising, but rising as a very personal expression to you. That is Ishvara. In the tantric teachings specifically, the techniques are associated with a particular Ishta. When one is doing the techniques that one is practicing, then that particular wave, that Ishta, arises and that expression is free from karma, free from all opinions, free from judgement, free from time. Then, you feel you have had a samadhi experience, a god experience. In the past, there has been confusion simply because they didn't have the technology, they just had ideas. If they had the experience of the infinite and in this experience the Ishta arose as a white, bearded man, then that was their experience of god. And if the intellect was not corrected, then god was a white, bearded man and stayed a white, bearded man. That is why it became a very popular idea, loosely based on some Italian painter's version of Zeus. The western version of god looks exactly like Zeus, the Greek guy; he is his twin brother. God is never black, he's always white, have you noticed that? In all the paintings, he's always white, really pale. This guy doesn't go out in the sun because he lives above the sun. I mean he should be brown at the very least, a compromise. In yoga, the tantric deities are a multitude of colors. Sometimes the goddess, or god, will arise in you looking blue, sometimes black, sometimes like a golden light, so you tune into that expression, into that golden light. When you are tuning into the expression of Kali, she may rise in that ferocious, dark indigo blue. God is not associated with one particular skin color. To have one particular skin color for god is so stupid. How could that possibly be?

What Patanjali is discussing here is the experience of unity consciousness. The experience of the unified field of consciousness at that deep level when one is experiencing and one is transcending space and time. When the consciousness rises as your personal god, your personal Ishta, she rises as your personal experience. The deeper you go, the more unique will be the form it rises in, depending on which specific mantras and specific kriyas you are practicing. It could be Chamundaye or Chinnamasta, the headless one with blood spurting out and her daughters drinking it, or Buddha who is rising from that unified field. Whichever it is, if you tune into that particular vibration, then your experience has that particular value.

तत्र निरतिशयं सर्वज्ञत्वबीजम् ॥ २५ ॥

*1:25 **Tatra niratishayan sarvajntvabijam***

The individual Ishvara, Patanjali says, is the seed of the limitless. Now, you be with that for a while. In the individual, Ishvara is the seed of the infinite. How beautiful is that? This guy is writing this not as a scholar, not as a writer. This is not his job. If you ask Patanjali, "What do you do?" He would not answer, "I'm a writer." He is a yogi simply sharing a profound experience. It is the natural response of a Master who is sharing with us. These are his deepest teachings and that is why they are so, so relevant.

स पूर्वेषाम् अपि गुरुः
कालेनानवच्छेदात् ॥ २६ ॥

1:26 Sa poorvesham api guruh kalena anavachchhedat

Patanjali says that this Ishta is the guru of all gurus. In the tantric tradition we say that the first guru, the origin of all the teachings, is Adiyogi Shiva. Even way, way back in the Rig Veda, what do we find? Songs of glory, songs to that which cannot be understood or limited by the mind. So what Patanjali is saying is that the origin of all these teachings is from this state. This is where the teachings are coming from, the individualized expression of the cosmic Being. This individualized expression rolls within its own consciousness and encounters the individualized expression of cosmic Being, downloads the teachings and shares them.

If you look at any of the great teachings, or even the great stories, they have come through many translations and interpretations and these interpretations take on many, many forms. So by the end of it, it gets very confusing. Like the three

Abrahamic faiths. The problem there is they didn't have the proper technology, so they all got a little confused and started fighting. Fighting a lot. But if you look at the story of Moses for example, this Jewish chap climbs up the mountain and he's alone, all by himself on the mountain top; he sees the burning bush and the storm comes. It is a metaphor; to think that this is real would be stupid. This poor chap, stuck up the mountain then has to carry this slab of rock down, without even a mule to help. And then the people at the bottom are just having a good time, having fun. Now here comes Moses, the party pooper, saying, "No, you can't do that. You can't have a good time anymore, God told me." He was not a popular guy. No, it's a metaphor; he is experiencing god within himself.

Thanks to the complexity of the Sanskrit language, these Vedic teachings have stayed intact and maintained their meaning. It stopped them from being diluted because they could not understand the language. These teachings are written in code. You have to practice them and as you practice them, only then do you understand them fully. All these traditions are talking about an individual having an experience within themselves and then bringing that teaching forward and sharing it. Someone has an insight, an event in consciousness, then the individual downloads it and shares it. So from the yogic perspective, Ishta is the guru of all gurus, Paramguru. That is why the form is Shiva Shakti. There is no one individual, no one single prophet.

That's the unique thing about the yogic teachings. They are not prophetic, no single prophet. They just come from all practitioners, people raising their consciousness, having experiences within themselves and sincerely devoted in realizing themselves, because these teachings are untouched by space and time. Therefore, when the yogi starts to practice, he or she is naturally bound to make contact with an expression of god within themselves. When somebody really meditates, really practices, they are bound to become spiritual. They might start off saying they're just using meditation as an aid to stress reduction, but if they really start to meditate, then they cannot just be interested in stress reduction. It is like someone saying, "I'm just going there to get a yoga butt." However, if by chance they really practice and stumble upon, by the grace of themselves, the subtler aspect of the teaching, it is bound to change the way they live. It can't help but do so, because that is the whole purpose of these teachings. You cannot remain the same. If you remain the same you are not really practicing, you are just fantasizing that you are practicing. There has to be change. Change will naturally start to occur; the way you see, the way you think, the way you give meaning to life, all of it will start to change. That's what the practice is designed to do.

So when Jesus says that the kingdom of heaven is within you, what he is talking about is that inner potential of Being. They just didn't have the proper technology at the time. Back then it was a case of either you agreed or disagreed. But you cannot base the truth on agreement and disagreement. If you do, then of course you're bound to run into trouble. Truth cannot be a matter of faith, faith is required in something that is not known to be true. If you don't know it, then you need to have faith in it; but if you can believe it, then you can also disbelieve it. So it is only the validity of your experience, what you can bring into your experience, that has value. If you cannot bring it into your experience, it loses its value. Here Patanjali is talking about Ishvara within the context of your own experience. When he says the guru of all gurus, he is not talking about a prophet, he is talking about the experience of going within oneself. From within, one starts to tap into what one's mind calls the mind of god, the unified field of knowledge and then one starts to receive that knowledge.

तस्य वाचकः प्रणवः ॥ २७॥

1:27 Tasya vachakah prannavah

In sutras 27, 28 and 29, Patanjali discusses the practice of mantra, using mantra as a tool within one's meditation to invoke certain experiences, aspects of consciousness, both within and without. Here he says, one of the sound currents is aum, the sound of silence. There are two values to aum. Within itself it has the flow state with a beginning, a middle and an end. The three aspects are manifestation, sustenance and destruction. The 'au' part is the infinity because it keeps going, the point value, localized expression, of infinity. For infinity is an infinite collection of points, that's what infinity is. You can only experience infinity within its point value, like time. Right now we are surrounded by the space-time continuum, but what are we experiencing? At this moment here, now, what are we encountering? We are encountering a point value of the infinity of space-time. So you can only encounter infinity within its point value and if you pay attention to the point value, if you can learn to refine the point value, then it will take you to a greater and greater infinite value, to corresponding celestial values of the grosser expressions of the point value. This progression occurs in stages: mundane to awake, cosmic consciousness, god/goddess consciousness, unity consciousness, the Absolute, braham sthiti chitta, you become one with god. Point value taking on its own cosmic value.

As one practices, one reaches a state where the inner Self is illuminated and the external self is illuminated. Like when you put a lamp in the doorway, inside the room becomes illuminated and also the outside is illuminated too, both values are illuminated. It is the same with this light of awareness, as it starts to expand within ourselves, we start to illuminate from the inside out, shining bright within and without. They are so very important, these sutras, and the way Patanjali describes it is really quite incredible. He is talking to us about Ishvara and he says there is no condition here. When we say free of space-time, we mean there is no condition. You don't have to be a certain way for god to love you. This conditional experience of god is purely politics, the politics of self-hatred, a way to keep people weak and feeling that they are never good enough. You find that this kind of conditioning even shows up for those who are practicing yoga, that they will deny the experience of unity consciousness, thinking that it cannot happen to them. "Me, have an experience of unity? No, no, it can't be, I'm making it up, I'm fantasizing. Am I going crazy?" They think they don't know what is going on, but actually they do know what is going on. They know exactly what is going on, but are too afraid to accept it, because if they do accept it then they have to let go of playing weak. Then what will happen to all the complaints? What will happen if they have to let go of all those narratives they have woven around themselves? The experience of Ishvara though, is not conditioned. It is accessible to everyone irrespective of their faith, their skin color, their socio-economic status, their education. It is accessible to everyone because it lives within everyone.

तज्जपस्तदर्थभावनम् ॥ २८ ॥

1:28 Tajjapas tadartha bhavanam

Here Patanjali speaks of the methodology of using the mantra. All the bija mantras that we use in the yogic tradition, in the yogic teachings, all have the value of aum embedded in them, the sound current of aum, aum being the primary sound from which all sound arises. Patanjali gives us the technique of using the mantra and invites the sadhaka to practice the mantras through the use of japa, the continual recitation of the sound and staying with the mantra, where the mantra starts to cancel out all thoughts. One then starts to move in the direction of the infinite meaning of that sound. For all sound arising from the infinite field of silence, all mantras of this yogic tradition, have unity consciousness embedded into them. When we stay with the mantra, we naturally find that the mind starts to follow the mantra and starts to have the experience of the meaning of the mantra, which is part of the great field of silence. Patanjali explains that japa is a very powerful technique, existing long before he wrote the Yoga Sutras. To refine one's consciousness and experience deeper, subtler states of consciousness within oneself, one must use the mantra with the proper technique, the proper power. The three aspects of the mantra are the attitude, the meaning and the tone. The three ways of speaking the mantra are vachika, which is when the mantras are said out loud through the mouth, the second is upanshu, where the mantra is whispered and the third is manasa, where the mantra is silently invoked within oneself, without any effort. All three techniques are relevant within the different contexts and we find the use of the mantra is a powerful tool in the yogic practices to achieve the subtler states of consciousness within oneself.

ततः प्रत्यक्चेतनाधिगमोऽप्यन्तरायाभावश्च ॥ २९॥

1:29 Tatah pratyak chetanadhigamo pyantarayabhavash ch

Patanjali is recommending that the student practice the mantra, the science of mantra, as taught in the Himalayan teachings. When the individual has been using the mantra to meditate, using japa, they start to refine their awareness by using the sound current. Then the individual starts to discover the meaning of the mantra. Using the right attitude, right power, right technique, one finds that one's awareness starts to follow the sound current and then one starts to have these experiences of the great field of silence within oneself. Simultaneously, as one dips into the field of silent consciousness, one finds spontaneous release of all obstructions, all distractions, spontaneous release of all impediments. So the experience of the inner field of silence, using the technique of mantra, allows the individual in that moment to transcend all impediments. All fluctuations are transcended as one allows oneself to follow the sound within oneself, follow the mantra within oneself, and start to experience the subtlest aspect of the mantra within one's own silent field. Then one experiences the pure field of inward consciousness.

व्याधिस्त्यानसंशयप्रमादालस्याविरति

भ्रान्तिदर्शनालब्धभूमिक

भ्रान्तिदर्शनालब्धभूमिकत्वानवस्थितत्वानि

चित्तविक्षेपास्तेऽन्तरायाः ॥ ३० ॥

1:30 Vyadhi styana samsaya pramada alasya avirati bhrantidarshana alabdhabhumikatva anavasthitatvani chittavikshepa stentarayah

Patanjali lists eight obstacles which can be commonly encountered, obstacles that are not specific to one individual but rather are a shared experience by us all. The first is vyadhi, sickness. not just of the physical body, but also of the mind, of one's consciousness. Sometimes people say it's the physical body and if the body is sick it cannot practice yoga. That is a misunderstanding. To think that people who face any physical challenge cannot practice yoga is simply not true. The practice of yoga, the techniques of yoga, can greatly benefit individuals who might not be experiencing an optimal state of health. The holistic practice of yoga will naturally bring an optimal state of health to us. As you practice, your health will start to radiate and support your practice more and more. So here, vyadhi is the state of consciousness which is dense on a physical plane, meaning unconscious living, physiologically, mentally, spiritually unconscious living. It is very obvious why unconscious living is an obstacle to the practice, the experience, and the state of yoga, because that state of consciousness is diseased, it is not at ease within itself. Physically it might not be optimal, emotionally it might not be optimal, on the level of its belief systems, it might not be optimal. So vyadhi here means the unconscious living, it is not merely physical health. It includes physical illness but, as I have said, that does not mean a being who has a physical challenge cannot experience yoga. That is absolutely not what this sutra means.

Styana is the second obstacle, styana meaning not interested. Again, it is very self-explanatory. If the individual is not interested in their evolution, he or she is not charmed by it, then there is not an intense desire. The desire has been hijacked by the ego and there is no desire, no perseverance, no consistency in the practice. They just practice every now and then, or once in a blue moon. As I always say, if someone asks you if you meditate and your answer is, "Sometimes," then you don't. It is like someone asking if you brush your teeth. "Sometimes" is not a good answer. So here, styana is that state when the practice is inconsistent, interrupted, or there is no real interest, no passion, no desire. These are all facets of ignorance that Patanjali is referring to. They are tamasic, meaning there is density dominating your consciousness.

Samsaya is when you are filled with doubt. At the dense level of consciousness, the individual is filled with doubt: doubt within themselves, doubt about the practice, doubt about their life, they are just filled with self-doubt, fear. In extreme cases, this can be paralyzing. But in a dense state of consciousness, there will always be the experience of doubt, a subtle level of anxiety. Samsaya is that indecisiveness, staying within the domain of doubt, self-doubt, self-hatred, having doubt toward the totality of life.

Pramada has two meanings. One is arrogance and the other is absent-mindedness, not being alert, the absence of continuous awareness, the absence of prajna. Prajna, of course, being continued awareness, the fifth quality Patanjali urges us to cultivate in sutra 20. So pramada is the absence of prajna, the absence of awareness. The individual in the dense state of consciousness is dominated by a sense of carelessness and arrogance. It is beautiful that this word has this dual meaning, one is arrogance and at the same time lack of awareness. Often, when the individual is stuck in a dense state of consciousness, there is a lack of intelligence, a lack of awareness, but there is an oversupply of arrogance. So it is a trap, a great trap. It is ignorant, but it is also arrogant in its ignorance. We can see that very clearly in our world, sometimes the more ignorant the individual, the greater the arrogance. That is pramada.

Alasya is lethargy, not having energy. In sutra 20, we talked about virya, energy, cultivating an energy-rich environment. Here the individual experiences alasya, an energy-depleted environment, not enough energy for life. That's why people start to drink energy booster drinks, because there is not enough energy to practice our sadhana, to live our life at an optimal level.

Next, Patanjali talks about bhrantidarshana. When one is not in the state, practice or experience of yoga, but is in a dense state of consciousness, then one might experience bhrantidarshana, stuck in an illusion. Bhranti is illusion, darshana is seeing. The individual's vision is dominated by illusion, projections. Fundamentally, they are looking at the world through rose-colored glasses, they have a distorted view and from that distorted view they give meaning to their life. Then, through the use of cunning tools and methodology, they maintain that meaning, safeguard that meaning, at any cost. The result is suffering. So bhrantidarshana is that state when the individual's awareness is dominated by projections, when he or she is not able to see the Is-ness of Is-ness but rather is bound by their projections. It can happen to anyone at any time. We can get lost within the projections of our own mind and really lose connection with the truth, with reality, but through the practice, through awareness, through alertness, we can transcend it.

Alabdhabhumikatva, instability, is the next obstacle; the individual is unable to maintain stability, is of an unstable nature, is ungrounded. In a denser state of consciousness, this quality is very present. Instability, meaning that you might well realize something, but if you're not illuminated and the dense consciousness is still dominating, then you will be too unstable to maintain it. It is important to remember that this is a quality of dense consciousness and not to take it personally. It's not you, it's just your state of consciousness and through the practice of yoga this can be easily transcended.

The last of the obstacles Patanjali talks about are anavasthitatvani chittavikshepa stentarayah. These two both have similar meanings. Anavasthitatvani means a continuation of the unsettled state, no stable state of consciousness, that the individual is very unstable within themself and chittavikshepa means to be distracted. So what he is saying is that when the individual is with him or herself, purely with themselves, they find it to be quite unbearable in their aloneness. They constantly need something to escape to, to run away from themselves. In the state of dense consciousness, the individual has no stable ground of being; they are lost in the doing and having, doing and having, doing and having. Whenever the doing pauses, the individual experiences instability and stress. They are constantly wanting to be in a state of busyness, of doing, in their mind and in their life. They find it extremely challenging just to be, without doing or having, just simply being. They don't see it as having any value. These are all expressions of a dense state of consciousness. In the absence of any experience, the mind becomes distracted, filled with all kinds of oscillating movements and the awareness fluctuates. They jump from one thought to another thought to another thought, a constantly moving mind, a constant background of white noise. It is like when you are surrounded with all kinds of electronic gadgets and you constantly live within that, your senses become oblivious to the noise they make because that noise becomes part of your life. Then one day, somebody comes along and switches everything off. All of a sudden, you become aware of a whole new dimension of silence. Then you realize that all this sound backdrop in your life was actually noise. In the absence of yoga, when this dense state of consciousness is dominating, the individual finds themselves stuck in this noise, this white noise of thought, this constant white noise creating stress. So in the absence of an illuminated consciousness, you will find that your capacity to be with yourself, without any distraction, any decoy or gadgets, without someone or something tugging at you, is much less. But through your practice and as you go deeper into yourself, you will find that your capacity to be with yourself, in your aloneness, will start to increase.

These are obstacles, Patanjali points out, that we need to be aware of but should not take personally, because they are simply facets of a dense state of consciousness and they can be transcended. It is important to be aware of that and not to feel defeated by them. They are not part of who you are. This is not the nature of self, this is the nature of consciousness when it is dominated by ego, dominated by ignorance. When you see these tendencies arising in you, do not judge yourself and go into self-hatred, but rather use your power of awareness to shine a light on them. Use the practice, anchor yourself in the practice and transcend, develop this constant capacity to transcend. As you go to subtler and subtler states of consciousness, move more and more toward unity, you will find that these tendencies naturally start to become less present within the field of your consciousness, less dominating, because your awareness is so alert now it has transcended them.

दुःखदौर्मनस्याङ्गमेजयत्वश्वासप्रश्वासा
विक्षेपसहभुवः ॥ ३१ ॥

1:31 Duhkha daurmanasyanggamejayatva shvasa prashvaa vikshepa sahabhuvah

In the previous sutra, Patanjali has discussed the obstacles that arise and that the practitioner must be very aware of them. Here he explains that if one is caught within the distractions and one starts to identify with those distractions, those obstacles discussed in sutra 30, then one finds that the accompanying experience is of suffering, of weakness. One feels weak within oneself, one feels grieved, the energetic body becomes weak, there is an energetic crisis that starts to happen. The prana is also affected, it is no longer smooth. The breath is no longer deep and fluid. Even the energetic system, the pranamaya kosha, becomes weak and an individual can experience an energetic crisis.

Often, when we find ourselves stuck in these experiences of grief, of feeling heavy, weak inside, feeling overwhelmed, unsure, uncertain within oneself, doubtful about our role in life or about the future, the human mind is then in opposition to itself and tries to fight these problems by looking for solutions outside of itself. Then one finds oneself in a trap. So it is of paramount importance that the practitioner, when finding oneself in these experiences, backs oneself with the correct knowledge. Instead of looking for a way out, we must be aware that all these experiences are temporary, they are not permanent. They are merely an experience that has accompanied an obstacle. They are just an outcome of being stuck in the distractions. One has lost one's way within oneself. If one just directs one's awareness back to oneself and dips into the practice, one can start to transcend these feelings. As we say in yoga, the only way out is in.

तत्प्रतिषेधार्थम् एकतत्त्वाभ्यासः ॥ ३२ ॥

1:32 Tat pratishedhartham ekatattvabhyasah

The way to transcend, the way out of this suffering that accompanies the obstacles, Patanjali says, is one-pointed practice. One finds that if you are stuck at any time, then in that moment, if you practice totally, you will be free. As the Buddha says in one of his sermons, if you practice this sutra for one month, you will be attaining Nirvana. Forget one month, if you practice for one week or one day or one moment, you will attain Nirvana. So the yogi knows that the only way out is in. When we are stuck in a distraction or the experience of grief or doubt or weakness within oneself, one should not waste one's time in organizing a pity party for oneself. One should apply oneself diligently, without wasting any time. Immediately one must apply the teachings and dive deeply with one-pointed focus into one's practice, into the teachings. Through this devotional practice, devotion toward one's practice, devotion to the infinite creative intelligence, one will transcend and move beyond these distractions and the accompanying experiences which arise from them. For a yogi, yoga is not something you do to get a good life. Yoga is who you are. Yoga is your life. Yoga is the experience that you have. Here, Patanjali stresses the importance of the state, the practice and the experience of yoga and devotion to that way of enlightened living.

मैत्रीकरुणामुदितोपेक्षणां सुखदुः
खपुण्यापुण्यविषयाणां
भावनातश्चित्तप्रसादनम् ॥ ३३॥

1:33 Maitree karuna mudita opekshanan sukha duhkha punya apunya vishayanam bhavanatash chitta prasadanam

This is very much a sutra for the times that we are living in. Here, Patanjali shares his insights into how we relate to others in our lives and in our practice. He says that through the cultivation of friendliness, compassion, reverence and indifference, there is a deeper progression on the path of yoga. Friendliness toward the joyous, compassion as in kindness in this instance, kindness toward those in pain, who are suffering or in sorrow. Reverence toward those who have realized themselves and indifference toward the wicked or those who are addicted to ignorance. Patanjali brings to the attention of the sadhaka, the student, these four ways of relating and urges them to cultivate these four qualities, four distinct expressions of consciousness that he or she will encounter in other people.

So friendliness toward happiness, toward the joyous. Patanjali is not saying that we have to keep looking for people who are happy. What he is really suggesting is that we cultivate a sangha, surround ourselves with people who are also working toward higher states of consciousness, because anybody who is moving toward a higher state of consciousness and devoting their lives to evolution, is naturally going to be moving toward joy as that is their essential nature. The essential nature of Self is joy. You will start to absorb the energetic field of that with which you constantly surround yourself. This should, of course, not be taken literally, we do not need to obsess about it. But when we have the opportunity, we should be mindful of all the company we keep and at least have certain individuals in our lives who have a shared intention of growth and cultivate meaningful connections with them. That shared intention of growth is naturally going to create an environment which is of joy. Here, Patanjali refers to joy not as pleasure, which is fleeting and based purely on a certain theatrical setting, but a state of consciousness which is able to maintain joy, radiant joy. This radiation of joy can only occur when the individual's happiness is not based on any particular circumstances, for happiness based on circumstance cannot have the power of radiance. It can only be a fleeting pleasure at best, one that is beginning, peaking and descending. Patanjali suggests we create a sangha as in the great teachings of Buddha, where he speaks of the three commitments that a Buddhist monk has to make, the Buddha, the Dharma and the Sangha. We must seek out our own tribe. This might not necessarily be people who are immediately surrounding us. They might not come from the same country or the same background or the same gene pool. These might be people who look very different to us, who don't share our history. But there is a certain connection, a certain resonance that we can start to experience together, a resonance which has a shared intention, a shared vocabulary, which is not dogmatic or closed off. It is open and naturally supporting and has an uplifting quality that each brings to the other's life.

The second quality is kindness, kindness toward those who are suffering. So we must first choose to surround ourselves with people who are consciously devoting themselves to evolving, because that commitment will naturally create a greater capacity for joy. Joy increases joy. When you meet joyous people you are infected by it. The more you surround yourself with that kind of energy, the more it will increase in you. From here, we can cultivate kindness and instead of judging and pointing fingers at beings who are in the state of suffering or a state of ignorance, we show kindness and ultimately that kindness will grow into compassion. The yogi will greatly benefit from cultivating loving kindness. It is a very meaningful practice to be loving and kind. Our world could really use this a lot. Whether we like somebody or not, whether we agree with somebody or not, whether we are pleased by somebody's presence or not, if we can cultivate the practice of loving kindness every day in our lives, if we intentionally practice loving kindness, in our behavior and in our vocabulary, then this world would be a much better place. It is not that difficult really, especially for those who are choosing to walk the path of yoga, seek yoga, practice yoga and be yoga. It should be a natural expression of our being to be loving and kind. Mind you, loving and kind here does not mean we have to be a doormat so someone can walk all over us. No, that's not what loving kindness means. Loving kindness means appropriate behavior when it is needed. If we practice loving kindness on those who are suffering, then it will really be established in our true nature. The practice of loving kindness in our behavior and in our thoughts is of immense value not only for our internal environment, but for the external environment of our planet as a whole.

The third quality is reverence. Reverence toward the wise. Reverence toward the realized. One must ask why does he use the word reverence? He uses the word intentionally of course, but it can be confusing and translated as friendly. Here though, he is not talking about friendliness. Friendliness he has already established in the first word, friendliness toward the joyous. Here he means reverence, celebrating the wise. When we are in a state of reverence, when we are reverent toward other beings, we immediately put ourselves in a state of receptivity. Not in a state of weakness, mind you, because this is absolutely not a state of weakness. In the yogic practice, the surrender or reverence we are speaking about is not one of the dogmatic kind but one that arises out of direct contact with truth. It arises from a very clear experience, not from some false belief system, but from a very clear state of experience when we have been touched by that light within us. You might think it is reflected from a source in front of you, but ultimately it is you. When we allow ourselves to get into a state of reverence, we are more receptive. So we cultivate this state of reverence toward those who have a certain degree of realization, those who might be vibrating at a level of consciousness which we might not be fully established in yet. This reverence has a function, it is practical. Everything in the Yoga Sutras has a practical meaning and is to be practiced. The practice of it will help you deepen your own experiences of yoga, the state of yoga which you have accessed. When we allow ourselves to get into a state of reverence, we are much more deeply receptive, we are able to receive the wisdom much more clearly. If you have a vessel and you want to fill this vessel with water but it has a hole in it, then no matter how much water is poured in, the water will keep on escaping and we will remain thirsty. This attitude of reverence, this attitude of receptivity, fills the hole in us and allows our attention to be focused, allows us to be present. When we don't have this reverence, our attention is fluctuating all over the place because there is a perversion of value on the subjective level. But when we allow ourselves to experience reverence and get ourselves in a state of receptivity, then there is a shift in our value. And wherever our value goes, our attention follows. Our attention increases and becomes focused, allowing us to receive and to absorb the true essence of the teachings, of wisdom, which ultimately is the very part of the very Self that we are. So we need reverence toward the guru, reverence toward the teacher, not friendliness, reverence, so that we are truly receptive.

The fourth one Patanjali discusses is indifference. Indifference toward those who are blinded by ignorance and are acting in a very dense manner. Here indifference is not apathy. Often people confuse indifference with apathy. Here, Patanjali is definitely not advising the student of yoga to be apathetic or to cultivate apathy. That is the total opposite of what yoga truly represents. Here opekshanan means transcending, going beyond, not letting the dense consciousness affect us, not letting it occupy our thoughts, not letting it occupy our consciousness. That does not mean that we are not able to hold it in our awareness. What it means is that the yogi is not dominated by an individual or a collective which is vibrating at a denser state of consciousness. When we do allow that denser state of consciousness to occupy the space in our awareness, it means we have given up our power and then it starts to dominate our life, affect our lives internally and externally. We are no longer able to practice. When you try to meditate, that feeling, that person, that thought, is constantly coming into your mind, almost possessing you. So here, indifference is not about turning your head away, it is about transcending the thought, reaching a state of consciousness where you are not giving away your power to an individual or a collective which is vibrating at a denser state of consciousness. That can only occur when you have no judgement about it, when you are neutral toward it and can see the Is-ness of Is-ness as defined by the nature of where the individual or the collective is at. Now you can rise beyond it and above it and that entity, that energy, is no longer possessing you, you have moved beyond it. From that location, whatever the appropriate action is will arrive. That action will be a response, not a reaction. Reaction never leads to anything good, reaction arises from the same dense state of consciousness from which the stimulus for that reaction arose. Tit for tat. It's actually the same thing. The tit and the tat are one. They are not opposites. They are not different. They are just spelled differently. Tit for tat is actually the same movement arising from a similar state of consciousness. So when a yogi is able to cultivate opekshanan, cultivate a capacity of transcendence over whatever they are being triggered by or finding toxic, as you transcend it and stop feeding it with your attention, you stop giving it your soul. Because whatever you give attention to will grow. If you keep giving your attention to it, it starts to grow and to consume you, to overpower you and you become weak. When you are not giving it your attention, you let your consciousness expand and you become aware of the infinite value that is available to you in every moment, even in this very moment. Do you realize that the infinite value of the cosmos is available to you, right now?

As you expand your consciousness and let your awareness and attention expand with it, then the individual or the collective which is vibrating at a denser state of consciousness is no longer dominating you. It no longer has any overpowering influence over your life, or your consciousness and from that place, you will act. Yoga is not speaking of inaction, not advising inaction, it is not apathetic. Yoga is advising you to take action which arises from a state of transcendence, take action only from that place. Patanjali says when we cultivate these four qualities, they will help us progress in the experience, the practice and the state of yoga, and deepen our relationship with the beings that we encounter in our life.

प्रच्छर्दनविधारणाभ्यां वा प्राणस्य ॥ ३४ ॥

1:34 Prachchhardanavidharanabhyan va prannasya

In sutras 1:34 to 39, Patanjali is offering us a slight taste from the vast reservoir of the yoga teachings and inviting us to enjoy the different practices. He elaborates on certain techniques to access the transcendent state and the refinement of one's own consciousness. He says the deep state of transcendence can also be accessed through working with one's prana. Here he explains how in the kriya tradition we work a lot with our prana.

When one uses these techniques of refining one's prana, one can access the cosmic mind. Through mastering one's prana by external retention and internal retention, refining all five of the different prana vayus: prana, apana, udana, samana and vyana, one finds that the mind naturally becomes still. In a being where the energy is restless, the mind cannot be still. When the energy is imbalanced, the mind cannot access stillness. So here Patanjali is inviting us to refine our prana, meaning the pranamaya kosha, the energetic field, that body of energy within our own energetic being. The primary access to this field is our breath, the only autonomous and non-autonomous function in the body. There is supreme value and power hidden in it. These powerful techniques, coming down through the Himalayan tradition, help access deeper and deeper states of consciousness and increase our capacity to embody higher states of consciousness. So this sutra is another clue, an invitation to some of the practices available to us, because obviously there is not enough space for him to share all the practices in detail. There are a lot of them with distinct techniques and distinct purposes. So here he is just referencing them, showing us that he is aware of the profound effect of these techniques. He makes a clear point, that this deep state of stillness is accessed through refining the prana.

The prana in the context of our breath has four parts: inhalation and exhalation, inner retention and external retention. Each different part of the breath has a different value and a different power. So through regulating our breath in different ways, we access different capacities and unlock the dormant energy within our body, within our being, which naturally gives rise to a clearer mind. The mastering of prana is fundamental in the path of yoga. Through regulating our breath, through uniting our capacity to be connected to our breath, to be attentive to our breath, we can access the no mind. Anchoring our awareness in our breath is a very powerful technique on the path of yoga. Through the different techniques, we find our resting pulse rate becomes lower and our breath rate becomes slower which naturally prolongs life. A resting high breath rate shortens the life span. Just look at mammals which have a high pulse rate, like a rabbit for example. An elephant has a lower pulse rate, lower breath rate and lives much longer. A normal human being can breathe 13-20 breaths in a minute. So through the practice of pranayama, the resting breath rate will always naturally be very low which makes us more present.

विषयवती वा प्रवृत्तिरुत्पन्ना मनसः स्थितिनिबन्धिनी ॥ ३५॥

1:35 Vishayavati va pravrittirutpanna manasah sthitinibandhini

Here Patanjali talks about the techniques of using sensory objects within the sensory perception to refine our capacity, whether it is using sound or objects or symbols. For example, in the state of pratika we use the yantra, or maybe a candle or the sound of the gong, to really access a deep state. In the yogic world of teaching, there is such a vast field of choice that ultimately all aspects of our life can become part of a meditation. So we can look at this sutra as an invitation to explore how even the sensory experience can start to become meditative.

Patanjali is also referring to specific techniques within the sensory perception to refine our awareness, refine our consciousness. Techniques such as the use of sound current, kirtan, the musical form of narration, or gongs, and so on and so forth. All these techniques and practices that are taught have different values but, of course, they all have a common theme, because it is through these techniques that one can start to access the silent field. These different techniques all have different values and purposes and yet there is a shared experience within them, but at the same time there is a distinction. One can use any of these techniques as an entry point and as one enters, one's consciousness will naturally start to expand. As one's knowledge grows, one will see how the different techniques are relevant to different aspects of one's being.

So, as I said before, Patanjali is just referencing the techniques. He is not really giving the details because the yogis who are practicing the Kundalini techniques know the different effects, different distinctions, different experiences that arise within one's consciousness. By using different values within one's sensory perception, it reveals to us that our senses are capable of accessing cosmic visions, even in the relative field of reality. For whatever exists in the relative field of reality, every sound, every shape, every form that we observe, is hiding a cosmic secret within itself. When we look at a flower, what we observe is a blurring phenomenon. A flower is ultimately localization of a non-local intelligence. What we actually observe is supreme intelligence, because hiding within the flower are all the elements, all the cosmic intelligence. For the flower to be a flower, there has to be supreme intelligence backing it. So as we refine our awareness of the flower, the flower is no longer a concept or a name. As we go deeper and deeper into the flower, that flower can be experienced in its cosmic form. Celestial value within a flower is ultimately the emptiness dancing at a certain frequency that is showing up to our particular nervous system as a flower.

Naturally, in the yogic teachings we have techniques and practices to refine the external experience. Our life is sensory and if we do not refine our sensory experience, then life can remain dull. By refining the sensory experience, life, even in the relative field, gains celestial value. A flower is no longer just a flower, a leaf is no longer just a leaf, a blade of grass is no longer just a blade of grass, a stream is no longer just a stream, a twinkle in an eye is no longer just a twinkle in an eye. Your experience of the variety of expression in nature starts to become much more fulfilling. Even in the waking state, the yogi starts to experience great unity. As Patanjali says, this is achieved through specific techniques and practices where one refines one's senses by using specific methodology. We can verify this from our own experience. When one is in a different state of consciousness, the same action, same experience, can have a totally different value. When one is moving in the direction of unity consciousness, then again the same actions will produce a different experience. So when you meditate with sound or a candle or kirtan, you get a different feeling, different experience. It's a vast field of different experiences, same fruit, totally different taste.

Patanjali invites us into the state of yoga, into the world of yoga. It's not just about the technique. He is not giving us the technique so much as he is showing us that he has heard about these different techniques. He has seen people practicing them and he is saying, "Look, there is this practice and also this practice and this practice." Of course, all these practices are guiding us toward the state of yoga, but he is saying that it's not like all roads lead to the same destination. You can verify it yourself. If you do Vipassana, you can have access to that state, but it's a very different experience when you have access to the state of grace of a guru. When you have a person touch you on the forehead, or actually embrace you, it is a totally different flavor. It's not the same thing. It is the same state, but at the same time it is different, because this field is so vast one can have access to different points, at different times and so have different experiences. Hence, there are so many different teachers doing specific techniques.

विशोका वा ज्योतिष्मती ॥ ३६ ॥

1:36 Visoka va jyotishmati

This is a beautiful sutra, quite beautiful. Patanjali says by invoking this practice, visoka va jyotishmati, by invoking the state of visoka, meaning sorrow-less, being without sorrow, and meditating on that state where there is no sorrow, there is jyotishmati, the state of inner light. Now, when we use this technique, focusing on the inner light, it has a different experience, a different value. If you are refined, you can immediately shift your state just by invoking that inner light. If we focus our attention and consciously invoke that state within our Self where there is no sorrow, the state of visoka, we are transcendent, a similar state to the experience of inner light.

Patanjali is very clear on this. He was practicing himself and he was using these different techniques in his own life, all this incredible, vast knowledge that is in the Yoga Sutras. Invariably, when you go into deeper tantric practices, you will start to have a very visceral experience of this light of consciousness, this inner light. You can invoke that through your awareness, you can invoke that vision through your intention. When we succeed in that invocation and that vision starts to spread itself in front of our consciousness, we find the mind naturally becomes silent and there is a great joy that starts to arise within our self, there is a natural elevation. Sometimes you can be using another technique. You might not even be invoking light, but all of a sudden, spontaneously, this experience can arise, the experience of inner light. You can verify this from your own practice. Sometimes you can close your eyes and you can say inner light and immediately it will arise. In that inner light state, there cannot be any thought. It's a thoughtless state but this thoughtless state has an inner glow because the conscious field has a glow, a faint glow. When your individual mind, individual awareness, accesses the field of pure chitta, it has a faint glow. So what we call this inner light is actually this glow of consciousness, the light of god. This light of god is the sorrow-less state because in this state there is no problem. There is only the state of "Don't worry, be happy."

वीतरागविषयं वा चित्तम् ॥ ३७॥

1:37 Vitaragavishayam va chittam

Patanjali now refers to the technique where we invoke Ishta or a guru as an ideal, as an archetype, to focus our awareness on and so move in that direction and embody that value. Again, if one goes deeper into the tantric teachings, one finds they are filled with very specific, precise techniques in the context of working with the different Ishta values of the Absolute, different finite values of the infinite. So naturally, if this technique is utilized in the correct manner, as one moves in the direction of the guru, or the Ishta, the mind can start to be filled with that value and one can start to find a great liberation through that state.

स्वप्ननिद्राज्ञानालम्बनं वा ॥ ३८॥

1:38 Svapnanidrajnanalambanan va

There are two meanings in this sutra. First, Patanjali is discussing the value of consciousness in deep sleep and the dream state. The individual has access to four states of consciousness. Deep sleep, which is the state of the unconscious. Dream state, the state of subconscious. Jagarat, awake, the state of wakefulness. Turiya, the transcendental state, the state of super consciousness. Here he talks about aspects of a specific technique. Just before going into sleep, when we are lying in bed, we can invoke maybe a certain sutra or a certain meditative practice. So even when you are entering the dream and sleep state, the awareness keeps on refining itself. The awareness can be present even in the subconscious and the unconscious state. For what we call these states of deep sleep and the dream state are all experiences on the level of the nervous system. It is the nervous system that is tired and stressed during its activities in the interactive relative value of life. It seeks to sleep, the rest of the body remains awake and functioning, the liver, the kidneys, the heart and so on and so forth. In the sleep state and dream state, the mind releases the accumulated stresses, but through the practice of specific sutras, even just contemplating the nature of reality before you go to sleep, contemplating the nature of soul, the atman, before you go to sleep, through that current, that contemplation can continue even when you are asleep.

For practitioners of yogic techniques, the physiology and the nervous system are infused with greater values of energy. They cease to be so easily exhausted, cease to be stressed. Through the practice of meditation, the nervous system reaches a deep state of relaxation even in the wakeful state. So in the state of sleep, there is a greater possibility of awareness being accessed. Sleep can be maintained but awareness can also be present. This technique helps us access a unified awareness without a break, a fluid awareness. The transcendental state can penetrate our deep sleep, can penetrate our dream state, and then our dreams can take on the value of astral dreaming, where they become teachers. Instead of the dream being the subconscious mind processing itself, we have access to supreme knowledge and of course, in the wakeful state we have a greater fluid awareness.

The other meaning is that as the yogi starts to be aware of the deep sleep and dream states, they start to realize that when the body is sleeping the seer is present, untouched by the sleep, untouched by the dream. Similarly, in the wakeful state, interactions with the relative reality are occurring, yet the seer maintains the untouched nature. Through meditating, contemplating the quality of one's experience through dreams and sleep and the temporal nature of all these phenomena, one can anchor oneself within the realization that even this awake state is also temporary, like the sleep, like the dream. One doesn't actually need to hold on to anything, any value. One interacts within this field that gives rise to the great value of vairagyam, detachment, within ourself. So by introducing a specific technique, a sutra or a mantra, before going to sleep, we really develop strong psychic powers, we develop strong intuitive powers. By using these subtle practices of the yogic teachings, of kriya and dhyana, our intuitive mind naturally develops greater strength and so makes the mind in the wakeful state attain a greater state of yoga unity.

यथाभिमतध्यानाद् वा ॥ ३९ ॥

1:39 Ynathabhimata dhyanad va

Through the practice of meditation and the different aspects of the yogic teachings, one naturally develops the capacity to be meditative. As your natural capacity to be meditative increases, you can meditate on any object that arises in the field of your awareness. As you are able to develop that capacity within yourself, a great clarity about any object that you meditate upon arises. Great knowledge reveals itself to you and the ultimate object becomes your own self-charm, the nature of your own self. All these practices rise to charm, to give bliss and then the term 'follow your bliss' starts to become true. Only somebody who has access to the natural state of bliss within themselves can follow their bliss. A being who does not have access to the bliss consciousness within themselves cannot follow their bliss. All they can follow is escape, all they can follow is pleasure, which is short-lived and can create a feeling of exhaustion over the long term. It can lead to a life of no impact, no purpose and no meaning and then a sense of emptiness can start to dominate. So one has to be very aware. In order to follow the bliss we need to first have access to that natural charm.

Again, there are two meanings to this sutra. First, that through the practice we naturally develop the meditative mind. Then any object which arises in the field of our awareness can be experienced with meditative awareness and it will reveal its knowledge. As the yogi gets deeper and deeper into stability, they are always in meditation. Moment to moment awareness starts to develop and any action, any activity that they are engaged in becomes meditative. This is a quality we must practice. This is a technique which we should be aware of, that we mindfully, consciously be meditative, be alert and fully engaged in anything that we do and do it like a meditation, like a spiritual sadhana. Whatever we do, even the simplest act, whether it is eating or walking or having a conversation with another person, every action has the potential to be meditative. For any object can become the object of meditation, total absorption can occur. When your meditation, when your yoga, starts to infuse every aspect of your life, the small, seemingly innocent actions of life, your whole life slowly starts to rise up and gain the value of unity and this is a life of yoga.

परमाणु परममहत्त्वान्तोऽस्य वशीकारः ॥ ४० ॥

1:40 Paramanu paramamahattvantosya vashikarah

Through the practice of the yogic teachings, the yogi starts to master their mind, master themselves. Through this self-mastery the yogi naturally develops the capacity to be attentive, from the subtlest thing to the grandest. The yogi's keen insight can penetrate the smallest detail and yet at the same time, the yogi becomes capable of being alert and attentive to the expansive, grand infinity of the cosmos. For the mind of the yogi naturally starts to take on the cosmic value infused by the celestial value. The mind becomes capable of being with the point value of infinity and the boundless value of infinity and everything in between. This gives rise to a special kind of knowledge, this capacity becomes extremely relevant in this life. It makes the yogi relevant no matter what role they are in, no matter what environment they are in. They remain relevant, for naturally they develop the capacity to understand every aspect of any situation they are in. For there are no complicated situations, there are only complicated people. When we say complicated people, we mean human beings who have not developed their inner capacity. This whole notion of complicated situations, "Oh no, there is too much going on, it's so complicated," these are words used by people who are stuck in their own weakness, stuck in their own victim identity. The yogi who can reach deeper states of consciousness can maintain the state of clarity in every situation, for they are capable of insight. Their presence makes the situation always better and not more complicated.

Insight should deliver us and the environment to simplicity. A lot of the time, what we find is human beings disguise their opinion in the clothing of insight. They confuse themselves because in the absence of training, in the absence of proper practice, one cannot have access to deep insight, for insight requires a deep silence within. So when we find ten people working together with ten different opinions, it creates too many complexities. We have to have the distinction between insight and opinions. The yogi develops insight, not opinions. Insight, relevant knowledge, the capacity to be with all from the minutest to the grandest. Most people want to do grand things, but they can't do the simple thing. They want to do a big life. They want to live large, but they don't have the capacity to have a great moment. If you cannot have a great moment, a great day, how can you have a great life? So naturally, the mind that is being refined by the practices of yoga becomes capable of being alert to the simplest, to the subtlest and to the grandest and the most intense. No work remains too big or too small for the yogi.

क्षीणवृत्तेरभिजातस्येव मणेर्ग्रहीतृग्रहणग्राह्येषु
तत्स्थतदञ्जनतासमापत्तिः ॥ ४१ ॥

1:41 Ksheenna vritter abhijatasyeva maner grahitri grahanna grahyeshu tatstha tadangjanata samapattih

Here, Patanjali gives the definition of the state of samapattih. He says that through the practice, the yogi experiences a unity within the three aspects of experience, the experiencer, the experience and the process of experience. The knower, the known and the instrument of knowing. The seer, the seen and the process of seeing. They are all ultimately expressions of one fluid consciousness, the seer is Self, the seen is Self and the process of seeing is Self. It is consciousness that makes it all possible. It is consciousness that sees, it is through consciousness that seeing happens and it is consciousness that is ultimately seen. It is that one supreme Being which is rising up in different values as the seer, as the seen and the field within which this whole experience is occurring.

Through the practice of the yogic teachings, applying oneself to these teachings, one starts to experience a great fluid unity. This state, this knowledge, when it starts to rise within oneself, is called samapattih, the state of fluid awareness. This gives rise to great power as the yogi realizes that the seer is the seen. Then we gain access to radical power within our self. For instead of fighting the seen, trying to make the seen change, the yogi fundamentally changes the seer. As a yogi applies oneself to this knowledge, the seer changes and so does the seen. Ultimately, as we reach toward this deeper state, we move in the direction of unity consciousness, the sense of self expands and the yogi fundamentally starts to experience the pure nature of Self, the pure field of consciousness. Within that, one experiences the whole cosmos as oneself, one's very own Self. This gives birth to the deepest compassion there is.

तत्र शब्दार्थज्ञानविकल्पैः संकीर्णा
सवितर्का समापत्तिः ॥ ४२ ॥

1:42 Tatra shabdartha jnana vikalpaih sankeerna savitarka samapattih

In this refined state of consciousness called savitarka samapattih, the word, the meaning, the content, all merge and a special kind of knowledge arises. This special kind of knowledge is savitarka samapattih, which the yogi naturally develops through the practices. As one refines one's consciousness, one is able to access this refined state and starts to be able to access the meaning behind the word. One is no longer trapped by the conceptual meaning. For god as a concept is very limited and ultimately creates divisiveness amongst human beings, as we have seen. But god as an experience is transformative, is unifying. So, savitarka samapattih is that state where we start to refine our consciousness, where we develop the capacity where the supreme knowledge, gyana, of any aspect of life starts to reveal itself in all its aspects, in all its levels, the level of the mind, the level of the heart, and then the level, ultimately, of the soul.

The conceptual meaning of the word is known, but so is the deepest meaning which is beyond the word and beyond the concept. Ultimately the celestial meaning is known. Any word, any knowledge, has three aspects, the conceptual, the experiential and, ultimately, the celestial value. At the celestial value, any object is ultimately that, but on a relative level it has a conceptual meaning, a meaning which exists purely on the level of human thought. For example, when we use the word rose to define an entity, an expression of nature that we call rose, this is a human word. It only exists within the context of the human vocabulary. It helps us to understand a rose on a certain level. Yet the word rose is not the meaning; there is a distinction between the experience of the rose and the word that is rose. Both are relevant, but the yogi has, through the practice of refining the state of consciousness, become released from the trap of the conceptual knowledge and has gained access to the deep wisdom. This access to the deep wisdom solidifies and helps the yogi progress and mature within their journey. But one must be aware that conceptual knowledge, in the absence of the deeper expression of that knowledge, is a trap and can lead one to ignorance. It is only through the practice and sincere devotion, refining one's intellect, correcting one's intellect, refining one's prana, refining one's consciousness, that one can have access to the capacity where one can transcend the conceptual knowledge. This is the true gyana that we must look for beyond the concept, otherwise we are trapped in the conceptual prison created by thought, it's a lot of words, but has very little meaning.

स्मृतिपरिशुद्धौ स्वरूपशून्येवार्थमात्रनिर्भासा निर्वितर्का ॥ ४३ ॥

1:43 Smriti parishuddhau svarupa shoonyevartha matra nirbhasa nirvitarka

As one goes deeper into one's practice, deeper into the state, the practice, the experience of yoga and the yogic teachings, the memory starts to be cleared. The intellect is now free from the conditioning of the memory and it naturally starts to become corrected, because it is anchored in the supreme knowledge, correct knowledge. An intellect anchored in correct knowledge does not create false meaning, false concepts.

Here Patanjali is explaining that the conditioning starts to be released. The memory conditioned through childhood, environment, mother, father, schooling, all these experiences and ultimately one's own personal karma, are released. Anybody who has been going into the deeper yoga practices can verify that this phenomenon is naturally experienced.

As we go deeper and begin to gain greater and greater consciousness within our own self, we become aware of the content which has been hiding in the realm of the subconscious from our conscious awareness. The yogi can become aware of memories that they may have denied. They can begin to see more clearly how that so-called trauma, so-called scarring, affects their behavior and leads them into a destructive path. The subconscious starts to bubble up and it begins to be released, thereby clearing the memory of toxic content. Then, the cleared memory starts to take on a celestial value and what we start to have is not a memory which is based in the past, but a memory which is based in the present. This memory which is based in the present gives us the capacity to keep hold of relevant knowledge, we do not need to be burdened by our memory. As this clearing occurs, our memory starts to become elevated. We can absorb what is relevant here in the present moment and we don't forget it. When the memory is filled with all kinds of toxic conditioning, the mind's capacity is limited. We may set intentions daily and by the evening, we have forgotten about them. A person gets up in the morning and says, "Today I will work out." By the time evening arises, they have totally forgotten about it and then they hate themselves and go to bed feeling guilty. This is because the mind is filled up already so it cannot remember properly.

Through the process of the yogic teachings, naturally the conditioning releases itself and the memory becomes free. Then instead of being about the past, this freed memory starts to be in the present, in the eternal now. It starts to gain more and more present awareness. The intellect is now backed by such a clear memory that it reflects pure consciousness and develops supreme power. As discussed in the previous sutra, a clear intellect gives us the capacity to be able to understand all that is here, to be with all that is here, the subtlest and the grandest without opinions, without projections, without complexity, only insight. We have to be aware that with insight will rise an accompanying sense of simplicity. The greater the genius in you, the more innocent you become and the greater simplicity you will experience. No matter how complex the world seems, when you are in touch with the creative intelligence, you will find simplicity in it. That is what gives rise to the flow state, meaning when the individual is expressing seemingly complex and nearly impossible tasks with utter elegance and simplicity. That is what we call genius, the flow state.

As the memory starts to be more in the present moment, it starts to expand, starts to give us access to the non-local mind. This intellect, now backed by the non-local mind, has memory that takes on the value of smriti, meaning having access to the cosmic knowledge. But first our memory has to be purged, it has to be cleaned. So one should not be surprised when things start to arise within you when one is on the path. These are all things which one has suppressed. One has to declutter the mind. One has to cleanse. It is part of the process. As the light of awareness illuminates all the samskaras hiding in the nooks and crannies, in the dark alleyways, all the cockroaches will come out, so don't panic.

एतयैव सविचारा निर्विचारा च सूक्ष्मविषया

व्याख्याता ॥ ४४॥

1:44 Etayaiva savichara nirvichara cha sukshma vishaya vyakhyata

Patanjali says that as the yoga develops within oneself both experiences of unity start to arise, savichara and nirvichara. Savichara is that state where the yogi experiences the full celestial value in the relative field of reality. Whether it is experiencing the great ecstasy inherent in the relative values of life, like the rose, the object is there. This is savichara, meaning with a thought. Nirvichara is that state where the yogi absorbs within themselves. There is no object remaining. The yogi moves within themselves and dips deeply into the pure ocean of bliss. In that great field of nothingness from where everything arises, ananda and asmita are experienced, sat chit ananda is experienced. Then we can have visions, movements arise, this is savichara. One can be in the deep state of deep purity and visions can arise. This is unity with vision, with movement. Nirvichara is that experience of unity which is accompanied with a total sense of void, emptiness is there; just bliss is there.

Through the practice, both values of unity consciousness become accessible to the yogi, savichara and nirvichara. When there is interaction with nature, meaning the world of the manifest, it is savichara. In the world of the unmanifest, in the great womb of the void, it is nirvichara. The yogi starts to have access to both these aspects and both are relevant.

सूक्ष्मविषयत्वं चालिङ्गपर्यवसानम् ॥ ४५ ॥

1:45 Sukshma vishayatvan chalingga paryavasanam

Here, Patanjali again discusses the state of cosmic consciousness. As one keeps refining oneself, one starts to gain greater unity with the manifest reality. The purusha and the prakriti merge; the self, the shiva and shakti merge. One experiences all that is and all that is not as one's very own Self and one starts to reach the pinnacle of self-realization. One has these experiences of oneself, one's cosmic Self, from within one's own meditative awareness. This experience within one's own Self, as one makes contact with cosmic intelligence, allows one to gain greater and greater unity with nature, thereby gaining support of natural intelligence. For when we observe, we realize it is nature creating and as we gain unity with nature, we gain unity with creative intelligence. All that is manifest is also consciousness. As I said before, all that we see and perceive is the dance of consciousness, shakti is shiva and shiva is shakti.

Great unity is gained and so this world of the manifest realm becomes infused with the great value of love and harmony. One doesn't need to escape this world anymore, for this world is nothing but an expression of the whole Being. It is only due to incorrect knowledge, bound by the limited mind and the ego, that we get confused and experience this reality as hostile toward us. Ultimately, all that we see and perceive is one's very own Self. This is a natural outcome of the practice and teaching of yoga.

ता एव सबीजः समाधिः ॥ ४६ ॥

1:46 Ta eva sabijah samadhih

This sutra is referring to the distinctions in the different experiences of samadhi: sabija and nirbija. Sabija means samadhi with seed. Seed of prakriti, of the manifest reality where one is interacting with the relative manifest dimension of reality and experiencing unity though that. The individual consciousness rests ultimately on the seed of that individuality, so it is the individuality experiencing unity. This individuality experiencing unity maintains its ultimate seed. The ultimate seed being the atman arising as individuality, the first seed, the cause, what we call the causal body. So even when one experiences deeper states of unity, that seed maintains, the individuality maintains; it expands, refines, evolves, yet it maintains. Even when the body drops, the individuality remaining maintains and enjoys its own manifestation, for all love is directed to oneself.

All these techniques of yoga help us access both savitarka and nirvitarka, savichara and nirvichara, sabija and potentially nirbija samadhi, where we touch upon the Absolute, where the I value just ends and there is just parabrahman. But we should not be concerned with that. We shouldn't be concerned with ending our individuality. We should be concerned with expanding our individuality, refining that individuality. Then this individuality is no longer in isolation. Individuality is ultimately an expression of parabrahman.

निर्विचारवैशारद्येऽध्यात्मप्रसादः ॥ ४७ ॥

1:47 Nirvichara vaisharadye adhyatmaprasadah

As the individual awareness starts to make contact with the source, there is a natural thoughtlessness that starts to arise. An absence of thought starts to happen, an absence of the constant commentary in one's head. Have you ever met the commentator inside your head, always commenting? As the individual continues their practice, they start to make contact with the source and the absence of thought starts to occur, the absence of analysis, and the commentator finally takes a much-needed rest. This absence of all disturbance, all distraction, gives rise to what Patanjali calls, nirvichara samadhi, meaning there is no more distraction and pure connection is experienced.

ऋतंभरा तत्र प्रज्ञा ॥ ४८ ॥

1:48 Rtanbhara tatra prajna

Once this pure connection is reached and the commentary in your head has ceased, then, Patanjali says with such beautiful imagery, the individual consciousness becomes filled with super consciousness, rtanbhara tatra prajna. It is filled with cosmic consciousness. Rtanbhara being cosmic consciousness, the cosmic field. Rtanbhara tatra prajna fills the awareness. You can verify this from your own experience as you consistently maintain this greater depth of silence in yourself, not only in the context of your meditation practice, but also when you are doing kriyas, asana or laya. When you go deep into your practice, this silence of thought starts to happen, this absence of self-commentary, and in that silence a unity experience occurs. This unity experience then gives rise to the individual consciousness taking on an incredibly intelligent form. Cosmic experiences start to arise in the individual and these cosmic experiences include one undoing or releasing the karmic baggage. A spontaneous release of the karmic baggage occurs and the individual awareness is able to maintain an undistracted silence. Now, this silence is not only the silence which is silent in the absence of sound. This silence means the contact with the potentiality of the pure field of consciousness. It is not stagnant, it is dynamic. You can see that even in a kriya practice. There comes a moment when there is no thought, no running commentary, no commentator. There is just the practice on its own. Then there comes a moment when even the practice is not there. The dancer is the dance and unity begins to happen. When you access that state, you can see it. You are doing a practice and sometimes you're right on the borderline. You are doing it and then you cross that line. If you are really paying attention, you can see this within yourself. Sometimes you will stay on this side of the line and maintain separation between you and the technique, but the greater you practice, the more you can see the line and so can quickly dissolve it. The moment you lean into the technique, thought disappears, the analysis drops, the commentary drops, the waiting drops, the critique drops. And what happens? There is a dynamic silence. This dynamic silence, when maintained, allows you to cross over the line, allows the individual awareness access to cosmic super consciousness, what Patanjali calls rtanbhara prajna, rtanbhara being cosmic consciousness, prajna, the field of awareness. They merge and what then arises is the experience. The individual starts to have an experience within that. Sometimes it is pure silence, you lose any sense of time. Sometimes it is a very dynamic experience. They can be emotional, they can be the absence of commentary. When one has a dynamic experience, one finds that immediately the analytical mind kicks in and wants to figure out what's going on. But the moment you try to do that, it goes. This fear of the unknown is there, this fear of loss of control, so at that moment one should just observe it and then one can go back in, cross back over the line. Through this crossing over, Patanjali says, the individual starts to have the experience of cosmic consciousness.

श्रुतानुमानप्रज्ञाभ्याम् अन्यविषया

विशेषार्थत्वात् ॥ ४९ ॥

1:49 Shruta anumana prajnabhyam anyavishayaa vishesharthatvat

Here Patanjali speaks brilliantly about the non-local knowledge. As the individual starts to make contact with this super consciousness, rtanbhara, it gives access to a special kind of knowledge, special because it is not bound by time and it is not coming through an object. Patanjali really is so brilliant. He says that this knowledge that one experiences is a unique kind. Usually the process of gaining knowledge has three aspects: the knower, the known, which is external to the knower and the process of knowing. When you study at school, for example, there is the knower and then there is the known. Whether it is biology, chemistry, economics, business studies, environmental sciences, or software engineering, and so forth, the nervous system is meeting an object external to it and then internalizing that concept within itself. But here this knowledge is a unique kind, it's a special kind of knowledge that is not object-derived. This knowledge is subject-derived and because it is subject-derived, one can not forget it. Knowledge that is object-derived one forgets. To give you an example, a toxic example, you can remember a toxic thought you had ten years ago, because it will be the same as the one you had three days ago. If you pay attention to the content of your thinking, you will find that the content is actually the same, it repeats itself. It's like you get new bricks and cement but you keep making the same house over and over again. The subtext remains the same. So here Patanjali is talking about the super knowledge, the super consciousness that occurs when the awareness, the individual awareness, starts to have the experience of cosmic consciousness. That is why it says in the famous sutra in the Upanishads, 'Know that by knowing which everything else is known.'

As the individual consciousness becomes filled with super consciousness and the individual awareness starts to have access to the special kind of knowledge, the experience that you have during your practice is also a supreme kind, because any experience has a knowledge attached to it. This experience that one has is not something that can be given to one. You cannot shop for it. You won't find it on Amazon. It is such a unique kind, one cannot just read about it or hear about it and it is difficult to explain. In the beginning, you find it hard to conceptualize it. Why? Because the linear mind has not developed intimacy with this experience. This experience is happening from beyond the memory. It does not have a memory, a reference, for this experience. So it is important when one is practicing and one is evolving and having this experience, that one not be in a rush to explain it within the concept of one's known concepts. Otherwise, what happens is one limits one's experience within the parameters of one's own history. As you have these experiences more and more and make contact with the source, in the dynamic stillness through your different practices, you will cultivate this level of unity consciousness and naturally start to have access to this special kind of knowledge, which includes intuition. Intuition is your capacity to remember the future.

Memory is remembering the past, intuition is remembering the future you would like to meet. We can verify this. The firing of the neurons precedes the behavior. The neurons fire first and then there is a slight gap, then the cognition of thought behavior. If the individual awareness starts to have access to super consciousness, then what happens? This super consciousness is triggering the neuron firing, not the past. So when we are doing the subtler practices in yoga, we are also changing the way we act with our physiology. We are taking charge over the decision maker. In the weak state, you are not the decision maker, the decision has already been made. That is why one finds one cannot help feeling a certain way. You wake up and you are irritated, you don't want to feel irritated, but you just are. If you were given a choice, if let's say there is a shop where you can buy different feelings, you would not buy irritated or annoyed. But one gets stuck in a state. So who is making the decision here, making the choice? Without this special kind of knowledge, one finds oneself helpless.

तज्जः संस्कारो न्यसंस्कारप्रतिबन्धी ॥ ५० ॥

1:50 Tajjah samskara anyasanskara pratibandhi

The consistency of having these experiences of unity consciousness or a transcendental experience, of cultivating this new level of consciousness and activating this new knowledge, Patanjali tells us, prevents new karma occurring, new samskara being created. When this intelligence has been set in motion, one finds one naturally starts to become free from self-destructive behavior, from cultivating self-destructive behavior. Otherwise, one finds it is quite easy to push the self-destruct button. It's actually a very easy thing to do. People do it unwittingly all the time. It's so easy that even when you don't want to do it, it still happens. So we cultivate this through the practice and as we have more and more access to this special intelligence within ourself, it then prevents the lower mind taking over our lives. Remember, the seed is only as good as the soil it is sown in. We have to get the best seed, but we must also cultivate it in the best soil. When both come together, when it is truly working, there is no having to wait for twenty years. There is a saying in India, if you left home in the morning and then you felt lost during that time, but you got back home in the evening, you were never actually lost. You were always on your way home.

A lot of the time what people now call yoga is just a word. There are people practicing for years, but what they practice is a very strange thing, just asanas and maybe a little meditation. The yogi practices the state, the practice, the experience of yoga. You have to cultivate the state. The deeper you go, the higher you rise. In the beginning you might find as you go deep, there is a little bit of darkness. A lot of people get scared and just remain on the surface. But, just like diving down into the ocean, as it gets darker the deeper you go, you have to adjust your eyesight, but the wave that rises from that depth has incredible power. As you go deep within yourself, so you too find there is less light there, but one has to face one's fears and still go deeper.

तस्यापि निरोधे सर्वनिरोधान्निर्बीजः समाधिः ॥ ५१ ॥

1:51 Tasyapi nirodhe sarva nirodhan nirbijah samadhih

Continuing on from the fiftieth sutra, here Patanjali says, tasyapi, when all the vrittis of the chitta are dissolved, the seedless samadhi, the nirbija samadhi, is experienced. This samadhi is a state of absolute transcendence which one can touch upon, but one does not maintain it. For if one were to maintain the nirbija samadhi state fully, then it would become braham sthiti chita and the physiology cannot maintain that state.

This experience of pure Being in its seedless state is experienced when the individual touches on it. Through touching on it, all the vrittis dissolve and the individual consciousness evolves from the mundane state to awake to cosmic, god/goddess, to unity, the Absolute and then to braham sthiti chitta, the highest. In that state, there is no individuality within the context of our experience.

But one finds that there is a choice here. There is a distinction between a Buddha and a bodhisattva, that being who chooses to maintain unity consciousness but does not surrender their individuality in the great womb of the absoluteness, because they feel a great charm in serving, in the uplifting of others, in showing them the way. So here, one only touches on this state where all vrittis are dissolved, all techniques merge and then one comes out of it. It is a touch-and-go kind of experience really, and that is what we want, that is desirable. If one stays in that state too much, then one is no more. So one cannot ever fully describe the nirbija state, because somebody who is totally absorbed in it is a nobody and braham sthiti chitta is lost forever. When Rama Krishna says in one of the stories, that I don't want to become my mother, I want to love my mother, he is speaking of god consciousness. That he wants to have that experience of Ishta as other, because there is a great joy in that, a great joy in experiencing the Divine as deeply intimate but also other. When you experience it for the first time, it actually shows up as something bigger than you. When you experience making contact with that pure field, that's why it moves you so deeply and tears can come. It is ultimately you, but there is a great crevasse and when that individual consciousness dips in, there is an incredible bliss there and we must cherish it.

So the nirbija state is that state of transcendence which one accesses through one's practice and techniques, where total merging happens. We make contact with it and then we return to the relative field. We make contact and we return, we make contact and we return, and our consciousness stabilizes and we evolve. Evolution of consciousness then moves through the different stages. You go from asleep to awake-fluctuating to awake-stable to cosmic-fluctuating, cosmic-stable. Just even a cosmic-stable is supreme enlightenment of this age.

Sadhana Pada

The word Sadhana means tuning, so here Patanjali is predominantly discussing the specific practices which tune our consciousness, tune our mind, and tune our body to experience the state of yoga. From the yogic perspective, our essential nature is cosmic, infinite. We are the localized expression of the non-local supreme Self. We are the time bound expression of the timeless. But when the timeless expresses within time, memory occurs and there is change, for change is time. As this individual value of self, the I, interacts with other relative values of self also within time, it forgets. It becomes entangled and develops complexities. It gets into a state of forgetfulness of one's own true, essential nature. Then it becomes stuck in all kinds of complex vibrations and as a result of moving away from the true wisdom, the correct knowledge, the entanglements become far greater. One goes deeper and deeper into karma, bondage, which causes the infinite Self to get stuck in a very finite, contractive experience which is fundamentally based in ego.

Here, in yogic terms, sadhana is used as a holistic word encompassing all the practices, the holistic practice of the yogic path which helps us to gain attunement with our source knowledge. It is like a musical instrument. If it is out of tune it doesn't matter how good a musician is, they cannot play good music. Even the greatest of musicians requires a great instrument, carefully selected for pitch and tone. Respected master craftsmen create these magnificent instruments, for it is the instruments of the highest quality which are required by the great musicians in order for them to play transformative, uplifting, deeply moving music. It is the same way for this individuality, this self as expressed in space and time. The body, mind and energy is an instrument which requires attunement, which requires disentanglement. As we disentangle and let go of the toxicity on the level of the body, toxicity on the level of thought, toxicity on the level of energy, we regain our essential nature and become attuned to the creative intelligence which is organizing everything around us. Sadhana, the techniques, the teachings, the path of yoga, helps us gain attunement so that the music of life can flow through us and this life can be lived as a dance and not as a burden. An individual who is not in a state of sadhana, who does not have access to sadhana, gets caught up in experiencing this life as an existential burden. None of us are interested in experiencing this life as a burden. We would all like to experience this life as a dance of bliss. So you can live this life either as a burden or a dance, but to live this life as a dance you must first have an instrument which is finely tuned. If the instrument is out of tune the music will be distorted, there will be only noise and no dance.

Sadhana is the supreme practice of the yogic teachings. As we bring this yoga into our life through our sadhana it allows us to be yoga, not just do yoga, but to be yoga and gain unity with the source, with our own essential nature, and so create a greater and greater state of flow in our lives. Like the bamboo, when full does not play music, but when it is hollowed out and tuned to create a flute, makes a simple breath into the most enchanting sound. Through the practices and the teachings of yoga, we release all the accumulated conditioning, all the accumulated incorrect knowledge and move deeper and deeper into our own essential nature. As we become emptier and emptier, the creative music of intelligence can flow through us and so our life gains the value of bliss.

तपःस्वाध्यायेश्वरप्रणिधानानि क्रियायोगः ॥ १ ॥

2:1 *Tapah svadhyayah ishvarapranidhanani kriyayogah*

Patanjali explains the four practices, or four aspects, of the path of yoga. Tapah has multiple meanings and the first meaning, the literal meaning, is tapas, heat, fire, intensity. When we interpret tapah in the context of yoga practice, it has three levels of meaning. The first, as I said, is passion, fire, intensity, that the yogi must cultivate a level of intensity in their practice. A level of passion, not only in their practice, but also in the way they live their life and a certain level of intensity in themselves, which is moving them in a powerful manner into the state of yoga. There's no half-assing their way through life. Whatever they are doing, they are doing it totally, fully, completely and absolutely. This is of paramount importance. If we are not fully present or engaged in whatever we are doing, we might as well not do it. It is disrespectful. If you are here, you need to be here totally, fully, completely and absolutely, in order for you to be able to experience here. That is the first meaning of tapah, this intense quality and presence with whatever you are engaged in. This passion is a quality we must cultivate.

Another meaning that arises within the context of our practice is self-correction, mastering our senses. Tapah and tapas can be misunderstood and mistranslated as self-mortification. That is not what Patanjali means. Yoga is not about injuring the body or feeling guilty and ashamed of our body. It is about the preparation of our body, but in an intelligent manner. Here Patanjali means self-correction. As you start to expand your awareness, you naturally start to witness your mind more clearly and the tendencies that arise within it. Now you see all the addictions, unconscious behaviors or dependencies that are there. You might have a certain ritual in your life that is unconscious. For example, maybe if you wake up in the middle of the night, you check your phone or it's the first thing you do when you wake up in the morning. It seems to be unconscious behavior, but when you witness it then you can start to consciously shift it. We are all people of rituals. Human beings are a species which has rituals whether they are mindful or mindless. We want to cultivate rituals that are mindful and let go of rituals that are unconscious and toxic, which are not serving the evolution of being. So the second meaning of tapah is self-correction, natural self-correction which arises from self-observation.

The third meaning that comes from tapah is a devotion toward our sadhana, toward our practice, where we cultivate a strong emotional feeling toward our practice, where it is not a means to an end. It is not a thing to be validated by or to show off that you can twist yourself into a pretzel. It is the way you live, it is part of who you are. You and the practice are no longer separate. You are the practice. The practice is you. You are no longer just meditating. You are meditative. Whether you are walking or you are listening or you are talking or you are eating or you are just staring into a child's eyes, or at a beautiful sunset or feeling the sand beneath your feet or going to serve the homeless or help the animals or serve the poor, ultimately you are serving humanity. Whether needy or not needy, actually, everybody needs help. So no matter what action is arising from you, you do it in a meditative manner. That intensity of meditation, where your meditation has become you, you are your meditation. Where you and your spirituality have merged, you are not just spiritual, you are spirit. That is tapah and is of immense value to the yogi.

The second quality is svadhyayah, meaning studying oneself, contemplation, reflection, self-observation and self-practice. Svadhyayah, the natural self-observation, the capacity to observe oneself without judging or analyzing, applauding or critiquing, is of the utmost value. That is svadhyayah and the ability to naturally be able to observe yourself is a direct reflection of your progression. The practice and experience of svadhyayah is to be able to naturally observe yourself, study yourself, be watchful, able to see your behavior, your thoughts, your tendencies, but without analyzing. When you see that you are able to observe without analyzing, without making a judgement, then you gain a greater clarity because in that natural observation there is self-correction. You begin to realize that this quality of self-observation is an indispensable aspect of your practice. If a yogi is not able to observe oneself without judgement or analysis, then there is no progress because they are still dominated by their senses and have lost focus. They are more focused on the objects in the earthly, mundane value of nature. Therein lies the trap, because whenever you give the object the dominant attention, you are then weakened.

The second meaning of svadhyayah is studying, developing a space in our life to deepen the wisdom that we receive, to contemplate, let it integrate into our being, let it assimilate. The third aspect is self-practice. In our world these days, we find that many people limit their practice to doing a class in a studio or at a yoga festival. Outside of that, the practice ends. Or it is merely for show, just so they can say they are doing yoga. So here Patanjali explains that the third value of svadhyayah is internal practice, the practice which is of value to you. It is the practice where there is no one watching, nobody looking at you. When there is no teacher or other students to impress, when social media is not looking, what is happening then? What is dominating the field of your awareness? What are you giving attention to when no one is looking? Self-practice, that is the third meaning that arises, but all three are of immense value. These are very important aspects which lead us into a deeper practice, experience and state of yoga.

The third aspect is ishvara pranidhanani. Ishvara means the sacred, the Divine, the higher Self. Pranidhanani means the absolute state of surrender. Devotion. Love. If we are not bringing the sense of devotion into our practice, then we are in our heads too much and the ego can hijack us. So this quality of devotion has to be cultivated. As I said before, devotion in yogic practice is not of the dogmatic kind, not worshipping some unknown entity, hopefully a god, sitting in a made up la-la land. Here, devotion is a quality which arises from self-correction, from your experience of something you already know, deep at the very heart of your Being. That truth is what you surrender to. So here, ishvara is referring to the very core of your Being. This very life is ishvara, this life is the Divine. The very breath that you just took is love. That inhalation, that exhalation, every beat of your heart is love. No matter how much our minds might try to reduce it, this life has an extraordinary quality to it that we know nothing about. It is incredible. Without you putting any effort into it, this prana is supporting you. This earth is supporting your body right now. All the five elements are carrying you with all of it existing to allow you to experience this very moment. It doesn't matter if it is challenging or if it is pleasurable, the fact is you are here. Ultimately, on an intellectual plane, you do not know exactly how many variables are connected to create this moment. So this life has a quality of mystery to it. Not a mystery as in some fantastical idea, but something which is very intimate to you. Yet the mind, which is based in memory, cannot fully understand it. That is ishvara pranidhanani. As we surrender to this incredible intelligence, it allows us to experience a deeper state of love, allows love to flow through us, allows love to love us. We don't fight against this love. We are not practicing yoga to fight the world. It is not the experience of me against the whole universe. It is you and the whole universe. Ultimately, you are the whole, the whole is you, ishvara pranidhana.

The fourth one Patanjali talks about is kriyayogah, the practice of kriya. Karma and kriya. Kriya is revolutionary action. Coming from the Himalayas, it is the Kundalini practice from the tantric traditions. These kriyas are specific techniques and practices which help us release karma, bio-memory, from our physiology and conditioning, from our nervous system. It helps us refine the value of our nervous system so it can open up to its fullest potential. As you go deeper into the state of yoga, the action that arises from you, which is supported by nature and is moving toward evolution, is kriya. Action that arises from ego, even if it is just asana, is karma, leading you toward bondage and limitation. Kriya is moving you toward expansion. It is the practice of kriya, the experience of kriya and the state of kriya. Our practice should be expansive, our practice should be integrated and whole, leading us into an expansive state of consciousness. It should not be reductionist and narrowing our state of consciousness. Patanjali uses the word kriya particularly to emphasize these specific techniques, the kriya techniques, from the Himalayan traditions. They are the subtle practices, subtle techniques, which help us release and let go of things that are not serving us and so help us to refine our nervous system to its fullest potential and take spontaneous correct action. This is the action which is evolutionary, which will help us transcend the karma, release it and move from karma to dharma, from bondage to expansion. When you infuse your life with kriya, the learning process quickens and the lessons that may have taken many lifetimes to learn, are learned quicker and quicker.

समाधिभावनार्थः क्लेशतनूकरणार्थश्च ॥ २॥

2:2 Samadhi bhavanarthah klesha tanukaranarthashcha

Through consistent cultivation of kriya, Patanjali says one starts to refine one's consciousness and thin out any obstructions to the experience of samadhi. The cultivation of kriya over a period of time starts to eliminate any obstruction to unity because unity is always here. Unless there is an obstruction to the experience of Samadhi, one should naturally be capable of experiencing unity consciousness but one finds one is not able to do so. It is because there are obstacles, afflictions within one's consciousness, so that it is not available to us. So here Patanjali talks about the cultivation of kriya practice to thin out the afflictions that stop the yogi from experiencing yoga and to take away the veil.

अविद्यास्मितारागद्वेषाभिनिवेशाः क्लेशाः ॥ ३॥

2:3 Avidya asmita raga dvesha abhiniveshah kleshaah

Here, Patanjali discusses the five fundamental afflictions in the state, practice and experience of yoga. The rule in Sanskrit is whenever you attach 'a' before a word, it becomes the opposite meaning. So vidya is knowledge and avidya is ignorance, wrong knowledge. Himsa is violence and ahimsa is non-violence. Patanjali says avidya, ignorance, is one of the biggest afflictions to the practice of yoga and is the fundamental cause of why the individual is not in the state of yoga. Asmita is ego, asmita raga dvesha, the three values of the mind. Asmita is the ego, raga is craving, and dvesha is aversion. If you start witnessing your mind, you begin to realize your mind is based in duality. It is constantly fluctuating between the two values of like and dislike, agree and disagree, I want, I don't want, I like this, I don't like that, I want this, I don't want that; it is constantly fluctuating in duality. So when the individual is living within the mind value, they are dominated by ego and the dual functions of the mind, thereby resulting in an experience of abhiniveshah, fear. Fear of loss, fear of death, fear of not being. Abhiniveshah, fear. So when you are staying within the mind, you are dominated by ego and then the mind, which is functioning in duality, is craving an aversion. If you begin to really see the mind, you will see that it is constantly busy. It is a mind which has not yet been refined and so it is constantly either wanting something or trying to shed something, constantly trying to figure out something or suppress something, constantly moving between these two extreme worlds. You are not your mind. If you are within the mind, you will fundamentally experience fear, abhiniveshah.

अविद्या क्षेत्रम् उत्तरेषां
प्रसुप्ततनुविच्छिन्नोदाराणाम् ॥ ४ ॥

2:4 Avidya kshetram uttareshan prasuptatanu vichchhinno udaranam

The field of ignorance, Patanjali says, is ultimately the cause of all suffering, the fertile field of ignorance. Avidya, ignorance, is the main affliction because it is the field of ignorance on which all the other problems, all the other afflictions, grow. So as long as the field of ignorance is there, if you're just trying to cut the growth down, it will continue to grow back. You cut one bush down and you say, "Ok, I have solved this problem and now I have everything I need in this life." Then you turn your head and, oh my god, something else has sprung up. Now you need to find a solution to another problem. You find a solution to that problem, you fix it and turn around again and there is some other problem. You think to yourself, if I could just get enough money, then I would be happy. You get that money and then it's some other thing. If I could be in a relationship, if I can just find my soulmate; you find your soulmate and there is some other problem, jealousy or ignorance or distress. We know this from our own experience. It is not the problems which need to be solved. It is the field of consciousness from which they are arising, because really the only kind of problems there are in life are ones which have solutions.

The reason human beings are incapable of finding the solutions to their problems is because of their state of consciousness. When ignorance is dominating the field of their awareness, their state of consciousness is in a state of ignorance; that is the root cause of all the problems. So here, when the yogi starts to awaken, they begin to understand the root cause of all the issues, all the problems of humanity. It is ignorance. We are ignorant. Why are we ignorant? Because we choose to be so. Do we have the possibility to transcend ignorance? Absolutely. But somehow we still choose ignorance over knowledge, true knowledge, not the knowledge of data and intellect. We're speaking of the knowledge on the level of soul. Patanjali really hits the nail on the head here. We are responsible. We are the root cause of the suffering of humanity. The answer is not to point fingers at others. This is an incredibly empowering realization when you understand it. If you are experiencing a problem in your life and you think that the other person is responsible, first take a look within yourself. You have the power to transcend. You have the power, the whole infinite universe is at your disposal. You matter, your state of consciousness matters. Stop playing at being weak. Rise up and claim your power. Let go of your addiction to constantly pointing a finger at others. Transcend the ignorance that you are holding on to in your consciousness and realize the true power that resides in your being. A mere drop of this truth can release such immense energy in you that the actions that arise from that place, will be of an incredible transformational quality in every aspect of your life.

Instead of fighting the problems we must, as yogis, deal with the root cause. Take away the field on which all these problems are growing and you realize they are not problems, but just an array of possibilities, a spectrum of consciousness. You will no longer be burdened by the affairs of the world. You can take appropriate action. You are relevant to the world. You don't run away from the world. You stay relevant to it, but you're not defeated by it. Spirituality is not about becoming a victim or becoming angry. These seem to be the two ways propagated by our society, to be either apathetic and just ignore it or to become a victim of it. That's not what we are interested in. As you recognize your true power, you begin to realize the invincibility of Self and that does not mean you run away. You stay relevant to the movement of the universe and the manifest world. Then, as your consciousness refines, your experience refines. There is your consciousness and the collective state of consciousness, but now your consciousness is the dominant force, your consciousness is the most powerful. Why? Because it is your consciousness. If you are in a dense state of consciousness and you are in the Valley of the Flowers, up in the Himalayas, you will still experience immense problems. "It's too cold. It's too wet. Why don't I have my guitar? Why is the sun not shining?" And so on and so forth.

When your consciousness is at a very refined level and you have transcended ignorance, you are able to see the Is-ness of Is-ness. What you are going to then focus on is the solution. You will bring in the solution. There are enough people in the world constantly pointing out problems, problems, problems. There's no shortage of people who can list the thousands and thousands of problems in the world. What the world needs is solution providers not problem providers. Solutions can only arise through a clear state of consciousness because ultimately there is only one kind of problem, those with solutions. They are the only problems that exist. Humanity is not able to find the solution to the problem because of their state of consciousness. They are looking at it from a particular state of consciousness which is biased, which is not ready to see the way, because really there is only the way. We are able to send people to the moon and yet we are not able to feed everyone. There is enough food to feed every little child on this planet. It's not a shortage of food. It is a shortage of consciousness, a lack of consciousness, lack of awareness, which is causing the shortage of food. We have enough knowledge. We have enough information. We have enough methods to feed every single mouth in a very optimum manner, but because our consciousness is dense, we don't. Patanjali points it out brilliantly. We keep looking only outward at the objective, when we need to go inward. He's not denying the external objective. Yoga is not about denying the external, but it is about realizing the internal and then the external will follow. Both have to be addressed, not just one value.

अनित्याशुचिदुःखानात्मसु

नित्यशुचिसुखात्मख्यातिरविद्या ॥ ५ ॥

2:5 Anitya ashuchi duhkha anatmasu nitya shuchi sukha atma khyatih avidya

In the sutra preceding this we discussed how avidya is the root of all afflictions, of all suffering, of all misery, because avidya is the incorrect knowledge. Here Patanjali defines avidya, or ignorance. In English, we often use the word ignorance to mean not knowing something, to be ignorant of certain information. But in this context, when we use avidya while discussing the root cause of suffering, the ignorance is not accompanied by an awareness of not having certain knowledge. This is ignorance in the context of having knowledge, but the knowledge is incorrect. That is why it is more correct to say incorrect knowledge rather than ignorance. Within the conditioned, myopic, bubble ideologies, it feels like knowledge, but it is bubble knowledge, disconnected from the essence of Is-ness, which is at the root of all suffering. It is a perverted ideology, the perverted state of relating to oneself and to nature. Patanjali sheds light on the nature of this ignorance and says that, in this context, the incorrect knowledge is to confuse the non-self as Self, suffering as happiness, the impermanent as permanent. All our afflictions arise from this perverted understanding of who we are and what this world is.

What are the fundamental questions? Who am I? What am I doing here? What is the purpose of life? Here the avidya, the incorrect knowledge, is our mistaken identity. The beginning of our ignorance comes from a mistaken identity of self, starting when the individualized consciousness became this finite expression of the infinite. The mind, the nervous system and the ego come into being. That is when we start to function through the ego and start to believe the ego is who we are. That is the beginning of ignorance, the beginning of self-hatred, the beginning of fear. A mistaken identity occurs, an assumption that you are what your mind is telling you, you are your thoughts. Your sense of self becomes based on the accumulated data that you have absorbed in your limited time here on this planet, encased in this bag of skin, but it is a non-self because it is not the full value of Self. You see, the Self is not only within the body, the body is also within the Self, within consciousness. Therefore, body is consciousness and so the full value of Self is pure consciousness.

When this consciousness is funneled through its individuality, then this individuality starts to express itself. Like the colorless sap in a tree. When the colorless sap starts to move in the direction of a green leaf, it starts to take on the quality of green. When it starts to move in the direction of a mango, it starts to take on the quality of a mango and by its mango-ness, it becomes limited. But if the colorless sap starts to believe, "I am only mango and that is all I am," it then tries to protect its mango-ness and starts to panic when the mango is about to drop from the tree. That is avidya, ignorance. The essential nature of Self is like the colorless sap and in that value, before it has moved in any direction, the possibilities open to it are infinite. But when the infinite crystallizes into the finite, funnels through this self, this finite value, it starts to identify the Self with the ego and that is the beginning of ignorance, confusing the non-self as Self. That is the root of suffering.

All our worries and fears arise from this mistaken identity. So for us to be fearless, we have to first understand that and then drop this mistaken identity. When the individual is dominated by fear, that fear leads to an imbalance and suffering, because the individual has confused the non-self as Self. Their experience of life is one of being disconnected, creating a constant anxiety. The individual then tries to give meaning to life. We start to limit ourselves, to hold on to ideas of who we think we are. We want to define ourselves through labels, religions, our relationships, through posts and positions, because we are always looking to define our identity, give ourselves a sense of self-worth. Instead of experiencing love, the ego is fundamentally experiencing fear and where there is fear, there is self-hatred. The ego is trying to hold on even tighter, not realizing that no matter how tight you hold on, it is impermanent because it only exists in time. Avidya is confusing the impermanent with permanent. As Freud said, humanity is collectively driven by a denial of their own annihilation. Human beings have a tendency to be in denial about their impending annihilation, push it to the back of the closet and lock the door. So they procrastinate in life, hold on to things. They don't know when to stop accumulating. It is quite insane. The funniest thing is that this insanity wears the mask of logic. It seems logical to the person because they are in ignorance, avidya, and because of this, whatever logic arises, comes from incorrect knowledge. No matter how insane the viewpoint is, the person who is holding that viewpoint will have enough logic or rationale to prove themselves right. We can see this right now in our world, very clearly. We don't have to look far. Every individual who has an opinion on this or that is able to prove why their opinion is the right one. This is ignorance, avidya, confusing the non-self as Self, the impermanent as permanent.

Patanjali also says we confuse misery as happiness. It is a brilliant point here. What does this mean, confusing misery with happiness? The yogi says that the individual suffers because somewhere within, they have chosen to suffer, to confuse misery as happiness. The nature of the mind is always to move toward joy. But when the person is in a dense state of consciousness, which is to say not in the state to yoga and mostly being dominated by ego, by the value of the mind, their perception of what will give them joy is perverted. A person who moves toward drugs, for example, thinks the drug is going to fix them, but in reality the drug is going to give them more pain. The idea is that the drug will give them some momentary freedom from their pain but actually it only causes more pain, so it's a vicious trap. It happens in our life all the time. We look for security. We create a bubble because we think if we're in that bubble, we will be happy. Of course, once we're actually in that bubble, it starts to suffocate us. There is a profound confusion, confusing unhappiness with happiness. When a person is in a dense state of consciousness, then their actions are moving them toward ignorance, toward pain.

Humans try constantly to find ways to escape their lives, their unhappiness, but why? Trying to escape is just ignorance. The solution is to expand. Gratitude and expansion of consciousness. That is why we are exploring the Yoga Sutras. You don't need to escape your life. You need to have correct knowledge to have wisdom. Once you are moving toward your true Self, there is no reason to escape. The need to escape drops away, it is replaced by a great bliss. Sat chit ananda. As your consciousness starts to expand and you start having access to cosmic states of consciousness, you start to become aware of the incredible bliss which is at the core of your being. You start to become aware that the value of Being is fundamentally blissful. Confusing the non-self as Self, the impermanent as permanent and misery as happiness, will fall away because these are all tendencies of the individual bound by ignorance.

दृग्दर्शनशक्त्योरेकात्मतेवास्मिता ॥ ६ ॥

2:6 Drig darshanashaktyoh ekatmata eva asmita

Here Patanjali, in his brilliant manner, discusses the ego. What is ego? In the yogic understanding, the ego is actually a projection within the mind value. The mind has three values to it, the fourth value is consciousness, but that consciousness is the power that infuses the mind with energy. When the three values dominate, there is ego. First there is manas, which is the accumulative mind. The mind accumulates knowledge like a sponge through memories and impressions, but when we talk about manas, we do not only mean on the level of the brain. We're talking about the whole body, the body has manas, has memory. That's why sometimes you might not remember what your grandfather or your grandmother looked like, but your body does. Their nose might be sitting on your face right now. You look at a picture and say,

"Oh my god, I look just like my grandmother."
Somehow your body has remembered. The second
value of the mind is buddhi, the intellect. The
manas receives the imprints and the buddhi gives
them meaning according to its conditioning, which
is ego or ankara, the third value of the mind.

Manas means the knowledge received through
the sensory organs. If you have sight, then your
eyes will be the overwhelmingly dominant way
data enters your brain. According to some
statistics, almost 80% of the data that an
individual is processing in their brain enters
through their eyes. When this information enters
the mind, the ego takes ownership of it, creating its
own false identity: I am Indian, I am a woman, I am
a man, I am pretty or I am ugly. Then all one's ideas
are formed by this identity. This identity created
by ego is a false identity, based on impressions
which the manas is receiving. The limited intellect
is trying to make sense of it. As it is making sense
of it, the ego is forming thoughts. Then something
tricky starts to happen. As the ego starts to create
a certain structure, it then starts to command the
intellect and now it starts to translate the data and
understand it from its own particular position. If
you present a certain experience to a group of
individuals, then according to their personality,
their ego identity, they will each have a totally
different take on it. This is ego, ankara, one of the
main afflictions to cultivating the state of yoga.

सुखानुशायी   रागः ॥ ७॥

2:7 Sukha anushayi raagah

दुःखानुशायी   द्वेषः ॥ ८॥

2:8 Duhkha anushayi dveshah

The dual nature of the lower mind is raga and
dvesha. Raga is the tendency of the lower mind to
constantly look for ways to escape, as Patanjali
puts it so brilliantly, to make this unbearable life
bearable. Dvesha is trying to avoid something,
suppress something, ignore something. The base
value of the ego is existential burden or existential
threat and because it is experiencing existential
threat, the ego is constantly looking for something
or trying to avoid something. It is constantly in this
duality, raga as craving or dvesha as aversion. I
agree, I disagree, I like, I don't like, I want this, I
don't want that, constantly in duality. It always
feels that it has to agree or disagree with
everything. Like or dislike everything. This is the
lower mind, the values of which are dominated by
the ego. It has a limited view and from that limited
view, it is constantly analyzing everything. But as
your awareness starts to turn inward and more
and more of the cosmic value of Self starts to
become available to you, then naturally this
overcomes the ego and you realize that you don't
have to agree or disagree with everything, like or
dislike everything, understand or misunderstand
everything. You rise above this lower value of the
mind and open up the possibility to explore and

make contact with the field of knowledge, the field of intelligence, which is much subtler than the lower mind. That is a great freedom, such a great freedom. When you realize you don't have to have an opinion about everything, then a great spaciousness opens up to you.

स्वरसवाही विदुषोऽपि तथारूढोऽभिनिवेशः ॥ ९॥

2:9 Svarasavahi vidush opi tatha arudhah abhiniveshah

Abhiniveshah means clinging to your way of life. This affliction of clinging to life, holding on to a lifestyle, is found even in the wise. This is a very subtle affliction, this holding on, and is a tendency of ignorance.

As you move into a subtler state of consciousness, you will start to consume more mindfully. You might become a vegetarian or shop for organic produce. Your behavior will be more liberal. All these shifts will start to happen as this birth of wisdom starts to occur. Then, after a while, it will start to become your normal behavior. As you are going into the transcendental state of consciousness, what we call cosmic consciousness, this behavior that made so much sense, this puritanism which might have arisen, or any new behavior which has arisen, is no longer of any value to you. As we continue to go into deeper states of meditation, deeper states of yoga, move more and more into unity consciousness, there will come a moment where who we have been, what we have been doing and the story our ego has written, no longer makes sense. It is not relevant anymore. In that moment, it has to be shed. We must let go of this old persona in order to move onto a subtler state of consciousness. All one's previous opinions, stories, codes of conduct, all of it must be let go because this mindset is no longer relevant, but even to the wise, it may still feel like it is. Now one must ask, why does Patanjali say that?

Even when you have awakened, there is a tendency to cling to this new, normalized position which has become part of your life. Then there is no longer any evolution. The individual hits a plateau and this is where that particular aspect of the ego, abhiniveshah, can develop, as Patanjali says, even in the wise. Why does he say that this particular quality is found even in the wise, this tendency to hold on? Because of fear. Patanjali understands that if it is hard for the wise to become unattached to life, just how difficult this letting go is for the average individual. He understands why the individual is not willing to transcend, to move beyond wherever they are and to go where they are not, yet they have been there eternally. What does that mean? In the beginning, when you transcend to another level, it will feel totally unfamiliar, but once you have become established in this new state of consciousness, it feels like you've been there forever. Why? Because in the absence of self, all levels of consciousness are available to you. It is all you, from the densest to the subtlest. So in conquering this attachment to life, one conquers the fear of death.

ते प्रतिप्रसवहेयाः सूक्ष्माः ॥ १० ॥

2:10 Te pratiprasavaheyah sukshmah

ध्यानहेयास्तद्‍वृत्तयः ॥ ११ ॥

2:11 Dhyanaheyas tadvrittayah

In sutras 10 and 11, Patanjali says that all afflictions, even the subtlest, even if they are only seeds of an affliction yet to germinate, can be transcended through the practice. Through our practice of yoga, through our evolution, we can start to transcend all our afflictions, all our conditioning.

Throughout our life, afflictions will occur, things which are just waiting for an opportune moment. Everything is fine, everything is fine, everything is fine... and then, boom! All hell breaks loose. That affliction was always there, lurking in a subtle form. It just needed a certain set of circumstances for it to be triggered and then it comes up to the surface. As we continue our practice and our evolution and the awareness continues to move toward the subject, instead of focusing outward on the object, constantly looking out through the prism of the mind, and the nervous system starts to refine itself, then the soul starts to look toward itself. In this movement, there is a crossover as, through the practice of yoga, you move away from these afflictions and you start to go beyond them, start to have access to the no mind, the cosmic intelligence. As you start to have access to this cosmic intelligence, you start to create distance between the Self and the mind value which is, as Patanjali has discussed, manas, conditioning, memory, karma. In this distance, this space, there is an awareness and you are able to see clearly and so transcend any affliction. Isn't that wonderful?

Patanjali is saying that when you go deep and turn your attention inward, that movement starts to burn away the stored kleshas, destroying them without them first having to rise and manifest in your life. But sometimes as they are dissolved, they are activated. Karma stored up, ignorant tendencies, stresses of life, unresolved issues. These kleshas which were hiding in the crevices just rise up to be deleted. When these kleshas are subtler, they are easier to transcend. Then, when the individual has to make a choice, instead of subconsciously creating a crisis so that they are forced into a decision because they are so afraid, the individual can learn and evolve. Patanjali makes the recommendation to learn quickly, otherwise we will not enjoy life. Once the field of ignorance has been removed, the fertile field of ignorance, where will the seeds of those afflictions germinate? Is this not absolutely brilliant?

क्लेशमूलः कर्माशयो दृष्टादृष्टजन्मवेदनीयः ॥ १२ ॥

2:12 Kleshamulah karmashayo drishta drishta janma vedaniyah

सति मूले तद्विपाको जात्यायुर्भोगाः ॥ १३ ॥

2:13 Sati mule tadvipako jatya ayuh bhogah

ते ह्लादपरितापफलाः पुण्यापुण्यहेतुत्वात् ॥ १४ ॥

2:14 Te hlada paritapa falah punya apunya hetutvat

In sutras 12, 13, and 14, Patanjali discusses karma and conditioning, our conditioning from this life or our past life. When the individual is not evolving, all that conditioning, all that memory, will affect our behavior and our state of consciousness, which in turn will affect the way we experience life, so it's a trap. A trap that goes on lifetime after lifetime. You see, when someone is not really evolving, they can just get caught up learning one lesson. Their whole life is about trying to learn one lesson. But as you go deeper into the practice of yoga, the full practice of yoga, there is a speeding up, a quickening, that starts to occur in you. As you start to learn the lessons quicker, you start transcending more quickly. The karma which might have taken you many lifetimes to transcend and to go through, starts to burn out much quicker. You start moving at an accelerated pace, moving to a much higher value. The karma doesn't have to be released at a grosser value meaning, because it gets released at a much subtler value meaning. If you are moving toward the grosser level, then the karma has to work itself out in a grosser manner. But if you are moving toward a subtler level, then the karma is worked out in a subtler manner, which is really much more fun, much more joyous. It makes life worth living, makes this manifest reality a magnificent place to be.

Through the practice of yoga, the individual starts to transcend this condition, starts to transcend dense karma. Now the karma is worked out in a subtler manner. If that is not happening, then the conditioning will keep repeating itself. The individual will be bound by karma, will keep moving into a narrower and narrower identity, feeling more and more isolated and disconnected from truth, disconnected from reality. How do we know where we are in our evolution? Well, it is the ego who asks that question. As you transcend the ego, you will become very, very clear and you will know.

परिणामतापसंस्कारदुःखैर्गुणवृत्तिविरोधाच्च
दुःखम् एव सर्वं विवेकिनः ॥ १५॥

*2:15 **Parinama tapa samskara duhkhair gunna vritti -
virodhaccha duhkham eva sarvan vivekinah***

To the wise one, all experiences that arise from a
lower state of consciousness are ultimately
leading to suffering. We find that the lower mind
is constantly busy creating aversions, constantly
stuck in duality. When one is at this level of
consciousness, at the dense state bound by ego,
one thinks there are experiences which are
pleasurable and experiences which are full of
suffering. One finds one is always busy trying to
escape the pain and chase the pleasure. One finds
oneself stressed in the anticipation of the pain or
suffering. The wise one knows that at this level of
consciousness, all experiences are painful. Even
those which one calls pleasurable are painful,
because all pleasure is a precursor to suffering.
The pleasure we seek just creates more desire,
creates more attachment, and that in turn leads
one to a deeper state of suffering. So the wise one,
the yogi, does not waste time in this chasing after
rainbows, but rather raises their consciousness.
As you begin to lift your consciousness, then
naturally you start to have access to that level
within yourself where these oppositions do not
dwell, where all experience does not lead to
suffering. To think when one is at a denser state
that there are experiences which are not going to

lead to suffering is simply not true. One can see this within one's own life. We can see it in our society and culture. People have much more now than they ever did. Everything they desire is fulfilled and yet they desire much more. Generations before, they did not even know some of the things that people now desire to possess. Yet we find that people are not any happier. They have all the gadgets, the phones and the yachts. Everything is there, but it is not enough. The pleasure is short-lived, the joy is short-lived.

Yoga is not against life or the fun of living. Patanjali is simply giving us the recipe for pure bliss. To the wise one he says realize that instead of wasting time chasing around for what one doesn't have, one must lift one's consciousness and discover the inner source. As one discovers the inner source, one rises beyond the field of duality. One is not stuck in the tug of war between pleasure and pain, chasing pleasure and trying to avoid pain. All pleasure ultimately leads to suffering. Only through access to a subtler state of consciousness, by using vivekinah, inner discrimination, can the wise one raise their consciousness, wake up their inner potential of bliss and radiate it out. Then one no longer clings to any experience, no longer denies any experience. One is open to all experience that life brings and one is able to live a life that is no longer in the pursuit of joy, but is an expression of joy.

हेयं दुःखम् अनागतम् ॥ १६ ॥

2:16 Heyan duhkham anagatam

Patanjali says suffering that has not yet arrived must be avoided. Isn't that a wonderful idea? Suffering should and must be avoided. How can one avoid suffering? One cannot avoid suffering by maintaining the same self. The only way to avoid suffering which has not yet arrived is by changing the self. Patanjali says whatever has happened has happened, but the future, which is the value of suffering that is coming, must be avoided. If the arrow is coming at you, you must avoid it, always get out of the way of the arrow. Don't maintain the state of consciousness that gives rise to the state of suffering. This suffering should and must be avoided. Patanjali is passionate in his kindness. He really wants us to get it. He is very direct. Look how passionate he is about it. Please, he says, avoid suffering. That's karma. If you maintain the self as it is, then the karma maintains its frequency. If you evolve, then the karma starts to turn to dharma.

द्रष्टृदृश्ययोः संयोगो हेयहेतुः ॥ १७ ॥

2:17 Drashtri drishyayoh samyogo heya hetuh

The union between the seer and the seen has to be transcended. Drashtri drishyayoh. What Patanjali is saying is, in the denser states of consciousness, the jiva, the atman, the soul, is identified with all objects that arise within the field of one's consciousness. So any thought that arises, any feeling or emotion, can totally hijack the individual. This tendency should be transcended, it should be avoided. If one is interested in living a life of mastery, living a life of yoga, then one has to be very vigilant of this tendency of the seer to be identified with the seen. This tendency to be identified with the content within the field of consciousness has to be first transcended, for as long as one does not transcend it, one remains identified with the content in the field of one's consciousness. Then one stays limited and this breeds suffering.

It's a natural outcome of the subtler practices of yoga that when we apply these practices we find this witness consciousness naturally starts to arise. The seer can then remain as the seer and not get identified with the seen. You can see it within yourself. The thoughts can arise but you are no longer bothered by them. You are no longer resistant to the thoughts because you are not identified with them. You can allow these thoughts to arise, peak and disappear. You can allow feelings to arise, peak and disappear. They are no longer overwhelming you, they are no longer overpowering you, dominating your field of awareness. It is a crucial point within one's evolution to develop this capacity to create a distinction between the seer that is oneself and the seen that is the content floating within oneself. To know you are the field of consciousness not the content which is floating within the field of consciousness. As you raise your awareness, then you find that content also rises within the field of consciousness and starts to be more evolutionary. But before the content can become evolutionary, one has to reach that level within oneself where one can create a distinction between the seer and the seen. Patanjali says that this tendency of getting identified with the content of the consciousness is a natural tendency from a young age. It arises in the soul that becomes identified with the content and then more gets fed into it. You are Indian, you are American, you are a boy, you are a girl, you are not good enough, you are ugly, you are fat, you are beautiful, you are unsuccessful, you are poor, you are rich, you feel bad, I feel terrible. All this stuff is just content. But we find that this content becomes embedded into the nervous system which then recycles it and so the soul remains identified with these thoughts, feelings and sensations. The seer then stays identified with the seen and remains a prisoner of the content of their consciousness. So it is of paramount importance that the seer remains as the seer and does not get identified with the seen. The practice of yoga helps us to develop this power, this super power, and not get identified with the thoughts, feelings, sensations, memory, any of the vritti, any content within the field of one's awareness. You can see in the deeper state that you can begin to cognize sleep arising or not arising as an experience, as the content in the field of your consciousness. With subtler and subtler refinement, you will find that you will perceive a lot more. You will be able to perceive a lot more within yourself without feeling the compulsion to take ownership of any of the content that is arising within you.

प्रकाशक्रियास्थितिशीलं भूतेन्द्रियात्मकं
भोगापवर्गार्थं दृश्यम् ॥ १८ ॥

2:18 Prakasha kriya sthitishilam bhutendriyatmakam bhogapavargartham drishyam

This is Patanjali's terminology for the three gunas. First prakasha, light, illumination, this is sattva. Next kriya, action, which is dynamic, and is rajas. And then sthitishilam, steadiness, which is tamas. So light, action and steadiness. Drishyam means the seen, that the drishyam has the qualities of illumination and bhutendriya means that it is tuned. So from Patanjali's perspective, the three gunas all contain within them prakasha, kriya and sthitishilam, which is a really wonderful way of using these terms. Patanjali has used them intentionally and it's a wonderful use of these words. It takes away the possibility of misunderstanding. He is saying that the gunas, along with the five elements and the five senses, in collaboration with the sixth sense, the mind, are what shape the world that is seen and experienced by us. It really is a brilliant insight. Now fundamentally, this world has two purposes and this is very important for us to realize. Patanjali says the objective of this manifest dimension of reality is experience, bhoga, but bhoga is experience which creates joy. So the twofold purpose of the manifest dimension of reality is celebration and liberation.

Now, these gunas are tuned to a particular nervous system. The world as we perceive it is the way it is only to our particular nervous system. To a nervous system of a rat, to a nervous system of a cat or a dog or a whale, this world is quite different. We often take our interpretation of this manifest reality as the ultimate, the Absolute, but that is a great folly. We have to be aware that this world of shape and form that we take for granted is only so to a particular nervous system. The dog does not come into the room and switch on the air-conditioning or look for the light. It tunes its senses to be able to see in any light. It is quite marvelous, the dog never wants to switch on the light. I play hide and seek with my dog. It's quite fun. I can tell him my hiding place and it makes no difference, but if I play with kids and I tell them where I am hiding then there is no game. It's all over. But kids can't see in the dark. The point is that the world that we take to be the Absolute is not really the Absolute. It is relative to our senses which are dependent on our nervous system. So here Patanjali with his genius is just giving us a little insight into the nature of reality, with its three qualities. Prakasha, light, illumination, that which is self-illuminated. Kriya, that which has movement inherent in it and sthitishilam, stillness within that movement. Dynamism and stillness coexist. That stillness gives the form value and the dynamism gives the growth value, so we find rocks can grow, mountains can move.

This world arises as content in the field of one's consciousness. It just arises. Everything this nervous system perceives is a blurring phenomenon. It is not the Absolute. If these eyes that we have had an optical nerve like a microscope, we would be seeing a very different world, wouldn't we? Or what if the optical nerve was like a telescope? You would be looking at a very different world indeed. Yet, we take this all as if it is the Absolute which, as I said, is a great folly. So here the great genius that is Patanjali gives us a little insight and clearly tells us that everything is moving, illuminated movement, but it also has a certain level of structure. The five elements, earth, water, fire, air and ether, in conspiracy with the five senses of action and the five senses of perception, channeling through the nervous system in the mind, give rise to the world in the field of the seer's consciousness and so to that which is seen and experienced. As you sit here and read this, or as you walk in a garden, or play with a dog, all that you see is a scene created by your consciousness. It's quite genius that this world arises only in the consciousness of the seer. And this world we, the seer, sees has to be enjoyed.

So no matter what you are doing, your intention is what? Joy and growth. To aid our growth, we have the gift of imagination. We like to imagine stuff. Let's say you have reached that level of harmony within yourself that you are only a little bit neurotic but not extremely neurotic. People who have an extreme sense of neurosis imagine all kinds of weird stuff, which leads them to punish themselves and go deeper into fear-based living. Anxiety and fear are merely a product of a faulty imagination. As I've said before, the mind can turn its gifts into its own weapons. But let's say you have reached a certain level where the neurosis is not dominating your wakeful consciousness so that you can imagine. What purpose does your imagination serve? If you can guide your mind willfully to not imagine all kinds of horrific scenarios, then what is the scene you would like to imagine? Surely something that gives you pleasure, joy, great unity. Imagine yourself flying, floating in the clouds. Imagine yourself on the mountain, merging in the light. But why imagine anything? For joy and growth. The act of imagination opens up the field of possibility. It's all coming from you but it opens up the possibility of another you, of all the yous you can imagine. Our imagination is there for us to grow and to expand, to enjoy and transcend our limitations.

The twofold purpose of the manifest dimension of reality, which arises in the field of awareness of the seer, is distinct in the human. This book is of little use to a dog and it is not a birthday gift you want to buy for a pig. If you want to buy the pig freedom so that he doesn't become bacon, the book won't help. It arises, but is only relevant for a particular nervous system. It is for our emancipation and celebration. You see, you must have a good time and you can only have a good time when you are free. When you are liberated, you are in god and god is always a good time. You can have glimpses of joy, but for a lot of people the joy of life is like an intermission from the suffering in both directions. It only happens on a vacation, when having a piece of cake, a smoke, or whatever it may be. That kind of joy is only a little break from the rest of their life, the real purpose of which should be celebration and liberation.

विशेषाविशेषलिङ्गमात्रालिङ्गानि गुणपर्वाणि ॥ १९ ॥

2:19 Visheshavishesha linggamatralinggani gunna parvani

Here Patanjali discusses the four aspects of the gunas and how they interact. Vishesha, meaning very isolated, differentiated, where one guna is dominating. Avishesha, where they are merged, undifferentiated. Alingga, a mere trace, there is no distinct identity yet the potential is there. And lingga, some movement has arisen, you can observe the gunas. They are not fully manifest, yet you can see little traces of it within the movement. In the dominant guna, you can see the tamas, the rajas or the sattva very clearly. Or, they can exist where the difference is not there and one is not dominating the others, they are more blurred within each other, avishesha.

These four stages can be applied to any content, for example, a thought. You can see the thought as a very clear, distinct thought, vishesha. Or maybe, you find sometimes you are sitting there and there is just the noise of thoughts. Somebody asks you, "What are you thinking?" and it is like, "I don't know." It's not like you don't know because you have no thought. It's just that there is noise going on in there. That is avishesha. Then the third stage is where you are not really thinking, but the thought is just trying to come up. You are not at ease. There is no actual thought, but there is a very slight feeling that something might come. This is lingga. Then with alingga, the potential is there for a thought but it is closer to silence, closer to transcendent consciousness. As when you go into a meditation sometimes, you can see the thoughts very clearly, then you see the thoughts just kind of merging and you can't really see what the thought is, but it's there. So four stages of the gunas, they can exist as very clear and differentiated, undifferentiated, when they are merging and when movement is there but it is not very distinct, it's only as potential.

द्रष्टा दृशिमात्रः शुद्धोऽपि प्रत्ययानुपश्यः ॥ २० ॥

2:20 Drashta drishimatrah shuddhopi pratyayanupashyah

Drashta, the seer, is pure consciousness yet the seer perceives through the mind. It uses the mind to perceive everything. Soul, body, mind. Mind, body, soul. Isn't Patanjali amazing? Drashta drishimatrah shuddhopi pratyayanupashyah. Ultimately, the seer is consciousness, the observed is consciousness, the process through which the observation happens is also consciousness, for everything that exists is only consciousness. Be with that for a moment.

The seer is consciousness, yet the seer perceives through the mind, hence the mind must be refined. To discount the mind altogether would be an act of folly. The seer is pure consciousness but if it perceives through the mind, the mind must be refined. You are a seer but in any moment, to perceive anything, you must go through the faculty of the mind. Your nature is consciousness, this consciousness is observing through the mind's eye and what it is observing is also consciousness. But without refining the mind, consciousness cannot be refined. You know this from your own experience. You can walk around practicing yoga, but you know secretly you must master the mind, refine the mind. Without refining the mind, no change is occurring. The seer, the seen, the faculty of seeing. The seer is consciousness, the seen is consciousness, the faculty of seeing is also consciousness. Patanjali is a genius.

तदर्थ एव दृश्यस्यात्मा ॥ २१ ॥

2:21 Tadarth eva drishyasya atma

That which is seen exists for the atma, the mind, to perceive and enjoy. The pracaryasya exists for paridrsta and paridrsta exists for pracaryasya. The seen exists for the seer, the seen exists through the seer. Like the observer effect in quantum mechanics, is it a particle or is it a wave? It is both depending on what one is observing. The classic Schrödinger principle, is the cat in the box alive or dead? It is both depending on when one is observing, both probabilities exist. The universe is constantly dividing itself into multiverses, with all choices equally possible and one can verify this from one's own experience. You make a choice and go down that road and you will meet real things there, it will not feel that it is in any way unreal. You make a different choice and again you will encounter real things, people and events. So the seen exists for the seer and ultimately the whole purpose of the seen and the seer are to unite and to realize the full value of the manifested and the unmanifested, realize it in its full value. That, Patanjali says, is one of the purposes of yoga, full value realization. The internal realization of the Absolute and the external realization of the

Absolute. Infinity within, infinity without. Shiva and Shakti.

This is verifiable from within our own cognition. When in those moments we experience yoga, we are successful and incredible, bliss arises. When we hold that bliss and open our eyes and move in the relative field of reality, we then find that bliss has a tendency to be shared. It likes to be shared. It does not want to hide away. It doesn't want to show off, but it naturally wants to radiate out. As you go within yourself and start to experience that inner state of freedom, what you find is that it can be maintained for a while. It is not just in an isolated event. When it is sustained for a while, it has a natural flow to be shared. It radiates outward without any effort. You naturally become more and more generous and more and more expansive in your external realm as well. I have found in my own experience that all the beings that I know to be accessing this inner field, to be in this state of yoga, have truly found that in their external realm they were very expansive, meaning that they could not be contained within their own parameters. A Swami I know who cleaned the floors could not contain himself within the identity of a floor cleaner. There was a genius in there. He was actually a retired engineer, he and I used to talk a lot about physics over chai with lots of sugar.

Naturally, as you start to become more and more fluid, the seen expresses itself so the seer can perceive it. What a beautiful thing that is! That is why the seer perceives through the mind. Look at the flower. The flower is God, God manifesting as a flower so God can enjoy God. God is quite narcissistic. A bird is singing. A bird sings because there are listeners. There is a perceiver of the song and there is a song. If there is no perceiver of the song, there is no song. For the song to be there, there has to be a perceiver of the song. If there isn't any perceiver of the song, then there is no song, but the singer of the song is itself the perceiver of the song. Without the perceiver, perception doesn't exist. If there is no perception whatsoever then the perceived cannot be, for that same faculty which gives rise to that which is perceived also gives rise to the perceiver. They are expressions of the same: the perceiver and the perceived, the observer and the observed. Now, be with that for a while. That is not to say that when you close your eyes there will be no trees. Somebody else is perceiving them too. Perception is maintaining them. The cosmic Being is perceiving them. For an individual, it begins with the perceiver is the perceived, the observer is the observed, the dancer is the dance, the experiencer is the experience.

Whatever you experience is a commentary on your state of consciousness. In this very moment, right now, you are having an experience. You are aware of both the experience and of having the experience, so there are two aspects to your experience. This experience is within the field of your awareness. The only thing you ever experience is your consciousness. Anything you describe as an experience is the experience you are having at any given moment and you are aware of that experience. When you talk about it, you are talking about it within the context of what your consciousness has experienced. All experience you have exists through your consciousness. You cannot have an experience outside your consciousness. It is not possible for you. You can have an experience beyond your present state of consciousness, in an expanded state of consciousness, but all experience exists within the field of consciousness, the seer, the seen and the process of seeing. If the seer is refined, the faculty through which the perception is occurring is refined and then naturally that which is perceived is refined.

There are those individuals who can walk through a magnificent rose garden but label it simply just a garden and walk on by. Then there are those who now find that they are in awe of such an expression of nature. Where earlier they too might have discounted it, now they are in amazement of it. The perceiver has refined, the faculty of perception has refined, so that which is perceived is now refined. As the Buddha says, meditate on the leaf. What he is saying is refine the perceiver, refine the tool of your perception and as you refine the tool of your perception, the leaf will reveal its secret to you, the perceiver, because the leaf contains all the secrets of the universe. The secret of creative intelligence is embedded in the leaf, it is an impulse of creative intelligence that has risen up as this leaf. We can verify this from the modern tools that we have. The base of this leaf is the field of nothingness, so this nothingness is rising up as this leaf. It is being perceived as this leaf by consciousness because consciousness, the perceiver, is perceiving through the mind, which helps reduce consciousness to observable boundaries. What one calls forms are the boundaries created to allow the seer to see the form. If you ask a physicist, they will say that all boundaries are merely concepts of a nervous system, because in reality there are no boundaries.

कृतार्थं प्रति नष्टमप्यनष्टं तदन्यसाधारणत्वात् ॥ २२ ॥

2:22 Kritartham prati nashtam apyanashtam tad anya sadharannatvat

In this sutra Patanjali says, as the seer, the soul, the atman, gains self-knowledge, they begin to realize their own essential nature as pure consciousness. The world that is then seen, the world of shape and form, does not get destroyed. It still exists and maintains its reality for it is a shared reality with different nervous systems. The indriyas, parts of the body, elements and gunas all still function in their relative values, even though they are but one point value of the individual value.

You can gain emancipation, gain liberation, through self-knowledge. That does not mean that the world totally fades into nothing. It maintains itself and so gives birth to the possibility of an ecstatic experience of life. For the seer, the being in illumination, can experience greater and greater enlightenment, the absoluteness of their own nature, while simultaneously interacting with the relative field. They are now anchored in the Absolute, anchored in the timeless domain within oneself, and also interacting with the world of shape and form. Sometimes there is a misconception that illumination or enlightenment is the end of it. No, it isn't. Enlightenment is the beginning of what we call awakening. It is not the end, it is the beginning of the play of life. For then, the twofold purpose of our world can be truly realized. What is that? Emancipation and celebration.

It is important for you to realize that, as a practitioner, when you are having experiences, the world, the relative field of reality, shows up in a very different way. Forms move, colors arise, energy dances, while to others it does not. If they have not yet had this experience, don't try to tell them what it should be like, because for them reality is still showing up tuned to their nervous system. Through the subtle practices of the yogic technique, it is natural at times for you, as you gain a greater sense of unity, to start to have these experiences where the elemental nature of reality behaves in a different manner, where you have visions and experiences and so on. But it is your vision and experience. For the majority, the classical laws of physics maintain, the nature of reality maintains. Even though you are having an experience that does not mean that now the whole world is like that.

Simultaneously, this whole idea that once you gain emancipation, once you gain a greater state of awareness, somehow you will cease to exist or become otherworldly; this is a myth. You don't become otherworldly, because there is no other world. This is a great lie, told by people who are looking to escape because they hate it here so much and they have manifested this other through their imagination, manifested a heaven, some place in the future where they will reach nirvana. There is no other place to go to, the only world to go to is here. You do not become otherworldly. You become more present here and your heart expands so you can maintain yourself as the absolute Being and anchor yourself in it.

One must remember that this is not necessarily something anybody else will understand. So if you're trying to make other people understand who you are, then guess what? You're not it yet, because you need validation. You still need other people to agree with you for you to believe in yourself. You only need other people to agree with you if you have insecurity within yourself. If you do not have insecurity within yourself you don't need other people to agree with you. It's a great relief. That's why I love mad people. They don't need anyone to agree with them. They are in their own world. They don't care what others think. It's really beautiful. My guru used to say, the mad and the enlightened have one thing in common. They are both out of their minds, they have their own individual consensus.

स्वस्वामिशक्त्योः स्वरूपोपलब्धिहेतुः
संयोगः ॥ २३ ॥

2:23 Sva svami shaktyoh svarupopalabdhihetuh
samyogah

Patanjali discusses the manifest reality here. Why the non-dual appears as dual, why the parabrahman appears as shiva and shakti, why the indivisible singularity, advaita, appears as plurality, dvaita. For there is an incredible power that the advaita seeks to experience, which it cannot experience unless it becomes dual. The power which we call Kundalini can only be experienced once there is manifest dimension, otherwise Kundalini remains dormant. In tantra, we give the higher seat to shakti, for the goddess Shakti holds the power. What is power? It is reverberation, stillness, pure consciousness, reverberation of consciousness, it is manifest. What we call subatomic particles, they are all coming out of what? Nothingness, this vacuum. But as this nothingness bursts forth, there is this incredible creativity. It gives birth to the possibility of experience, to the possibility to evolve, to experience itself in this incredible variety.

So the purpose of life is for you to evolve, celebrate and realize. When we say realize we mean grow, to be moving in the direction of self-realization, the ultimate value of Self being infinity, braham sthiti chitta, infinity consciousness. There is immense power that arises through this expression of advaita and dvaita, advaita meaning the non-dual, the indivisible whole, ultimately maintaining its indivisibility. This manifest reality maintains its indivisibility, yet it expresses itself as divisibility. But even though it is expressing itself as divisible, it is indivisible. It maintains its indivisibility, that is the incredible beauty of it. The whole maintains the indivisibility of it, yet it arises as plurality. Singularity maintains and plurality arises. Why does it happen? Patanjali explains that it is because this dance of shiva and shakti has incredible potential in it and this potential is a revolution, this potential is of experience, infinite experience. For the infinite can experience itself back in infinite ways.

Within the manifest space and time, you have the potential to grow, to evolve, become wiser, become kinder, more appreciative, humbler, if you are in the right state of consciousness. Or it can go the other way, the possibility is there but one has to be willing to explore the possibility, otherwise the experience remains one of suffering. The supreme Being wants to expose this possibility of experiencing the incredible potential power which lies inherent in it, dormant in its singularity yet expressive in its plurality, in shiva and shakti, to explore the possibility of this ecstasy.

तस्य हेतुरविद्या ॥ २४॥

2:24 Tasya heturavidya

Now in this sutra, Patanjali looks at why this duality happens and what makes it occur. For individuality to arise there has to be what? Time. Without time, there cannot be individuality. What we call time is a blurring phenomenon. It requires a very limited nervous system. If we had a cosmic nervous system, we would experience no time because we could take all the particles and all the probabilities into consideration, so time would cease to exist. For there to be time there has to be change, this change is what gives birth to time. For individuality to be there, there has to be time and this time is what? Maya, illusion. This is the grace of the goddess, manifesting herself as the illusion of space-time. Some think it is a curse to be here, but there is a great ecstasy in being here. Only the lower mind thinks it is not, but actually we know deep in our hearts, there is a great joy in being here. It is the blessing of Maya.

Here Patanjali is using avidya in a different way. This avidya is not ignorance, but self-forgetfulness, that one has to forget the singularity. As the wave arises from the womb of the Absolute, it has to have this element of forgetfulness. Why? Because there is time. It is entering within space and time and time is what? Memory. There has to be a beginning and for there to be a beginning there has to be a clean slate. That gives birth to the indivisible whole, the Absolute. The timeless can play within time. It's where you and I can happen, though we are ultimately Aham Brahmasmi, the Absolute. I am That, but you and I can play as this, we can tango and jam and play cricket, share some bad-for-you-dessert together. When the forgetfulness maintains itself and the process of remembrance, of evolution, is not started, then it leads to suffering. This forgetfulness, hand in hand with the process of remembrance, results in ecstasy.

तद्भावात् संयोगाभावो हानं तद्दृशेः

कैवल्यम् ॥ २५॥

2:25 Tad abhavat samyogabhavo hanam tad drisheh kaivalyam

Patanjali says if this forgetfulness does not become chronic, then it does not maintain itself forever. The forgetfulness for the whole will maintain itself, but if the individuality within that field can avoid this chronic ignorance, then the union can maintain, can arise. Union being what? Yoga.

The experience of separation is nothing more than an illusion. Subatomic particles kind of prove that because even when they are separated by space and time, they behave as if they are twins. They are connected by some invisible force, for if you do something to one the other behaves in the same way. There is no separation, yet there is what we call separation. It is a blurring phenomenon at the level of our senses which makes life the way we live possible. If there was none of this blurring, how could there be you and I? There is a great ecstasy in the experience of you and I and we, but one has to realize that this is a blurring phenomenon that is occurring. Otherwise we could not experience boundaries, without which there would be no individuality. There is joy in boundaries, of course, but only if you know they are not real. If we believe in boundaries too much, then we fight. If we can maintain the awareness of the boundary yet at the same time be boundless, then we can enjoy and love and serve and uplift each other. We can cooperate and collaborate and not be an asshole.

So, hanam here is avoidance. Avoidance of what? Suffering. And suffering can be avoided. As Krishna says to Arjuna in the Bhagavad Gita, the cessation of suffering is yoga. The purpose of life is not suffering, but it can manifest. Why? Because there is forgetfulness. But it can be avoided. How? Through yoga. Set the course toward remembrance.

विवेकख्यातिरविप्लवा हानोपायः ॥ २६ ॥

2:26 Vivekakhyatiraviplava hanopayah

Vivekakhyati, unfluctuating awareness, continuous awareness, is the crowning jewel of wisdom. As you apply yourself to the practice, this awareness of your essential nature moves from fluctuating to stable and the stability of awareness expands as you gain your own cosmic awareness. As it becomes stable, it is called vivekakhyati.

Continuous expansive awareness is essential to liberation and maintaining hanam, the avoidance of suffering. So for you to suffer, you have to give up what? Your essential nature. You have to believe in your isolated identity. You have to believe yourself to be a bag of skin floating around in a hostile universe. You have to believe in the narrative of who you are. You have to believe in the fear. You have to believe in the insecurities that you have. You have to believe in that voice if it says you are not loved. All these are lies. Continuous awareness is liberation itself. If you are love, what is the need for anyone to like you or not? It's just absurd, right? Vivekakhyati, continuous awareness.

That does not mean you won't be challenged. Of course, you will be challenged, but there is awareness, continuous awareness, moving toward greater and greater unity, emancipation, and celebration through vivekakhyati, through applying ourselves in the practice of yoga. As we commit ourselves to the practice and the practice becomes our life, there is a natural stabilizing of awareness that starts to happen. This stabilizing of awareness keeps us from getting caught in our old patterns. Otherwise, the old patterns will keep arising and they will catch up with us. It won't matter whether we think we've done it all, read all the books, done all the sutras and the mudras, we will still find ourself in our own personal purgatory.

As you apply yourself to the continuous practice, the practice and experience merge. As you stabilize, then even when you do fluctuate, if you continue the practice the fluctuation will lessen. You will of course have your dips and find yourself in the familiar territory of your old patterns, but these dips will lessen if the practice is continuous. We shouldn't be surprised by these fluctuations. We should not judge them. The fluctuation is a natural phenomenon of growth which occurs as you move in the direction of stability. It is not a mistake, it's a sign of progress. As long as you continue the practice, then you will start to stabilize and that stability gives birth to the ability to not get hijacked by total forgetfulness. The clarity maintains, even though you might have thoughts of negativity. The temptation to go to a pity party might arise and sometimes you might go, but you will know you have an option to leave it anytime. Vivekakhyati, the continuous stable awareness that arises naturally as we apply ourselves to the practice.

तस्य सप्तधा प्रान्तभूमिः प्रज्ञा ॥ २७ ॥

2:27 Tasya saptadhaa prantabhumih prajna

As this stabilizing of one's awareness starts to occur, one starts to progress through the seven stages of enlightenment. As we start to stabilize, the individual consciousness starts to expand and this expansion makes us move to higher and higher stages of awakening. Patanjali explains here that there are seven stages of awakening, of illumination.

There are different interpretations, but the two we use are: first, deep sleep, second, dreaming, third, waking state, fourth, transcendental, fifth, cosmic, sixth, gods/goddesses, and the seventh being unity. Above that there are the eighth and ninth as well, the Absolute and Parabrahman, braham sthiti chitta, the Absolute merging, the end of duality.

It can also be expressed in a different way. The first stage is the ego state, the second is awake state beginning to go beyond the ego, the third, cosmic going beyond individuality, the fourth gods/goddess consciousness, the fifth is unity, the sixth is the Absolute, then braham sthiti chitta, the formless/shapeless. They can be expressed in both ways. The consciousness starts to expand through these stages of illumination, meaning greater and greater stability.

योगाङ्गानुष्ठानादशुद्धिक्षये ज्ञानदीप्तिरा
विवेकख्यातेः ॥ २८॥

2:28 Yogangganushthanad ashuddhi kshaye jnanadiptir a vivekakhyateh

Patanjali reminds us about the necessity of the practice of the techniques of yoga. He says that through practicing the different aspects of yoga, we naturally start to release the impurities, the toxins, from our consciousness and greater and greater illumination starts to arise. The spiritual knowledge, gyana, starts to fulfil us and give us greater and greater freedom and ecstasy. Yogangganushthanad is devotion, discipline, toward one's practice. Anushthanad is a devotional word, a sacred word. It is a very refined and noble word in the Sanskrit language meaning something you do consistently, but you do it because you are devoted, it's a devotion, it's sacred.

Patanjali is inviting us to have a sacred reverence toward our practice, to consistently apply ourself to the teachings in a sacred, devotional manner. Not in a dry, disciplinarian manner, nor by diluting it or cheapening it, but that we should apply ourselves to the great depth of the yogic knowledge and teachings with a reverence. Yogangga, applying ourselves to all the aspects of the technology, all the limbs of the yogic technology, to stabilize ourselves in the supreme knowledge, supreme wisdom, helps us evolve, grow and fulfil our purpose here, to self-actualize and self-realize.

यमनियमासनप्राणायामप्रत्याहारधारणा ध्यानसमाधयोऽष्टाव अङ्गानि ॥ २९ ॥

2:29 Yama niyama asana pranayama pratyahara dharana dhyana samadhayah ashtau angani

Ashtau angani, the limbs of yoga. Here Patanjali for the first time discusses the eight limbs of yoga. He is making a very important distinction though. These are not the eight steps to yoga, as most people translate them to be. These are the limbs. Just as your left hand is not a step to your body nor your right leg. They are all part of your body. Your right leg is your body. Your left hand is your body.

So when Patanjali is describing these eight limbs of yoga, he is actually talking about the being who is in the state of yoga and who is radiating these eight qualities. He then goes on further to classify and describe these distinct expressions of the being within the state of yoga. There are three levels to these eight limbs, the state, the practice and the experience. But don't think of these eight as distinct or separate from each other. They have to be approached in unison. Yama, niyama, asana, pranayama, pratyahara, dharana, dhyana and samadhayah.

The yamas and niyamas are talking about the quality of states of consciousness. They are not moral codes. In the Yoga Sutras Patanjali has been discussing something very profound: cosmic states of consciousness, the nature of reality, the nature of the mind. It would be quite ridiculous to think that after describing all this incredible depth of wisdom, Patanjali then gives a lesson in morality. This is not what yoga is about, it is not teaching morality. The yamas and niyamas are not moral teachings, but they are qualities that it would be wise to cultivate.

अहिंसासत्यास्तेयब्रह्मचर्यापरिग्रहा   यमाः ॥ ३० ॥

2:30 Ahimsa satya asteya brahmacharya aparigraha yamah

Patanjali addresses the five yamas, the first being ahimsa. As I have said, the rule of Sanskrit is that when you attach an 'a' before any word, it becomes the opposite. In Sanskrit, himsa is violence, ahimsa is the transcendence of violence. A lot of the time, when people encounter this first yama, ahimsa, they brush it aside, thinking, "I'm not violent, so this isn't really something which I need to explore." But here Patanjali is talking about the state of non-violence. A being who is not realizing their unity consciousness is, on a certain level, violent. As long as you are bound by any identity, whether it is your nationality, whether it is your religion, whatever it may be, on a certain level, you are going to be in conflict. If you believe you are Indian or French or Lithuanian, then on a certain level, that identity is at the root of a certain conflict. If you believe you are an American, that you only think like an American and you smell like an American and you see like an American, then ultimately, at a certain level, that identification with that identity is going to give rise to violence. Primarily, ahimsa is the state of unity consciousness. Only a being who is realizing their essential nature, who is moving in the direction of unity consciousness, of yoga, has access to non-violence, because it is a natural aspect of the yogic state of consciousness. Why? Because you are experiencing unity, experiencing love. As I have said before, when you are experiencing that love, then naturally you are going to be radiating peace.

People can sometimes be confused by the first yama being the transcendence of violence, because one of the biggest scriptures on yoga, the Bhagavad Gita, is set on the battlefield. The protagonist, Arjuna, is a disciple of Lord Krishna who asks him to take action, the action being to kill. Patanjali is discussing ahimsa, non-violence, but in the Bhagavad Gita, Arjuna is being asked to take radical action which involves shooting arrows at people he knows. Clearly, Patanjali is not just propagating the moral codes of pacifism here. He is talking about a much greater and subtler state of consciousness, a consciousness where natural unity is being experienced, because only then is the individual naturally radiating non-violence, experiencing non-violence. Even if an action which arises from the individual appears violent, the energy behind it isn't, because they are in a state of unity consciousness. That is important for us to realize. In the Bhagavad Gita, Krishna tells Arjuna to establish himself in yoga and then take action. Establish himself in yoga first. From the yogic state of consciousness, which is unity, from that unity state of consciousness, what arises is the law of nature, not of violence.

When Patanjali is talking about ahimsa at its highest level, it is the state of unity consciousness, because from that place, when you are filled with love, there is naturally going to be non-violence. If the situation requires you to be ferocious, you will be ferocious. If the moment demands you to be absolutely like a rabbit, you will be like a rabbit. When the moment demands you to be a butterfly, you will be a butterfly. If the moment demands you to be a lion, you will be a lion. That's why in the tantric deities, Durga is riding on a lion, Kali has a machete and blood dripping from her mouth, whereas Ganesha is smiling and Lakshmi has a lotus in her hand. All these values are distinct expressions of states of consciousness. Sometimes that ferociousness is required not only on an external level, but on an internal level too, to transcend your own inner demons, to face yourself fully. So here non-violence is not pacifism; it is an intense quality which arises, a quality of great courage, great power. Only the truly powerful can be non-violent, it is the weak who are seduced by violence. The truly powerful have a natural state of non-violence in them. This non-violence does not mean pacifism. It does not mean being a doormat. It means that when you are at the state of unity consciousness, then the appropriate response becomes available to you. Notice that I say appropriate response. That is not reaction, but response, the appropriate response. You will take spontaneous correct action; that is dharma. Krishna tells Arjuna that wherever there is dharma there is victory, yato dharma tato jayah. From that state of consciousness, unity consciousness, there arises spontaneous correct action. When you allow nature to move through you, to fulfil the purpose that it needs to, that is ahimsa, the state of ahimsa.

As yogis we want to practice non-violence in our actions, in our thoughts, in our belief system, in our identity. We want to explore how we are bound by our identity, because if we are bound by any identity, then we are contributing to violence. Being aware of what we do, being a witness to our behavior, we learn to observe and see if the behavior is arising from ego. Because ego is always in a state of violence. Why? Because ego fundamentally exists in a state of fear, it is always trying to control and is constantly concerned about me, me, me, in a reductionist, isolated manner. It is judging and critiquing the whole world to find a certain level of validation for its isolation. That is profound violence. My master used to say, there are only two kinds of non-violent people in this world. The majority are the first kind, the people who have not yet been pushed by circumstances to be violent. Their non-violence is not of a self-realized quality; it is just an accidental non-violence, a byproduct of a certain karmic situation. The moment you turn the situation around, change the circumstance, the violence which has been sitting dormant will then arise. The second kind are those who are consciously aware of their own potential for violence, who understand that the human species is inherently violent, that we are part of a particular species which is profoundly prone to violence. Which means that naturally there is that potential within us all. To just assume you are non-violent and not explore this possibility within yourself is an act of violence in itself. Yogis are consciously aware of their own capacity for violence and transcend it through their practice, through the practice of ahimsa, through their observation, through the way they live their life. The practice is an aid to transcending it as your ego comes into check, you drop the judgements and your attachments. Your self-hatred, self-sabotage, all this violence toward yourself, starts to drop away. You stop constantly shifting the blame onto somebody else, shifting the burden of responsibility onto somebody else, of always playing the victim role. You see, these positions are all violent, violent to oneself.

Ahimsa, the state of ahimsa, the practice of ahimsa, also affects our consumption. We become more conscious of our consumption, how we consume, how we chose to spend of our money, our time, how we are impacting the planet. Ahimsa is non-violence toward ourselves, non-violence toward our planet, non-violence toward our fellow beings. Apathy is violent. It is not by being non-violent that you move deeper into the state of yoga. It is by being in the state of yoga that you are able to achieve non-violence, it occurs simultaneously. If a being is not experiencing any yoga, they cannot be non-violent, it has to be a simultaneous process. Through the whole practice of yoga, you experience an opening of the system, the opening up to this value of self to love, to the cosmic value of Self. As this awareness opens to the cosmic Self, you are naturally making contact with the field of love; you are naturally transcending ego. As you transcend, you are able to observe your own tendencies, the violent tendencies within you, the unconscious behaviors that create violence and conflict toward yourself as well as to others. Are you open to the experience of this love? Or are you bound by the noise in your head? Because when you are bound by the noise in your head, then you are being violent to whom? To yourself. Complaining and whining about your life, about who you are, critiquing and judging, holding on to the pain and the victim stories, is being bound by your ego.

As you become really alert, you begin to surrender toward what Is. From that place arises appreciation for what Is. Now the correct responses, not reactions, will start to occur. You can only respond when you are not resisting what Is. If you are resisting what Is, you cannot respond, you can only react. So naturally, if you are in ahimsa, there has to be a natural gratefulness, a gratitude, for what Is, the things you like and the things you don't like, because you have access to expansive reality. You are not bound by a myopic vision, a vision of being that is created solely by your ego. One little situation which your mind is totally absorbed by, that's a perversion of perspective. No matter how challenging it may seem, there is always so much to be grateful for. Everything else is just the stories in the mind. This is violence toward self. Do you realize this? All there is is right now, this grace wanting you to experience this love, longing for you to experience it. And if you're not experiencing it, then why not? Who is responsible? Is there somebody controlling you? Is there somebody with a remote control deciding what happens to you? Lay down your weapons now and allow the love to fill you. We are not speaking of weapons in a literal sense. We are speaking of the weapons we have inside us, the walls we build to separate us, the armor we put on to protect us. From what? As you surrender to what actually Is rather than to what is imagined, this fearlessness arises and a great freedom is born. This is the state of yoga, the state of non-violence, the experience of non-violence, the practice of non-violence. It is essential to you, to your being. Can you, in this moment, be non-violent to yourself, to your life? Right now and in the greater value of now, what does it mean to be non-violent to yourself, to your life? Can you appreciate this moment in your life? Can you allow yourself to be present, here in this life, in all its mystery, right now? Without trying to reduce it just to certain enjoyable qualities, to control it, to manage it. Can you be non-violent? Can you practice non-violence?

As you practice this non-violence, you realize your essential nature is non-violent, that is who you are, that is the true value of Self. The state of yoga is non-violent because it is filled with bliss. Bliss consciousness, available to you right now.

You are either in love right now or you are in fear. You cannot be in both. Let the love transcend and conquer the fear. This is natural non-violence. You deserve it. Your heart deserves it. Break down the walls. Take off the armor. Live life fully. To not seize the great opportunity of life, to not live fully, is a great act of violence. Be filled with awe by this life you are experiencing, this great mystery that you can enjoy. That is love, a mysterious love, you can feel in every breath. Who are you? Why is this breath choosing to move through you? Are you just the story of this body? Or are you willing to catch a glimpse of your own true nature? You deserve to experience non-violence. All the beings on this planet long for it. Be a contributor to the value of peace, to the value of love. You can only be a contributor to the love value when you allow yourself to experience that value. You can only give what you have; if you don't have yoga, you cannot give yoga. Remember Arjuna and Krishna and decisive action. This non-violent action is the action of the strong, the wise, not of the weak. The weak make noise, shout and scream, behave out of fear. Non-violence requires courage. Sometimes, as you truly start to radiate this non-violence, this compassion, there might be some people triggered by it and start making a lot of noise directed toward you. We have to know that it is totally fine and not personal. This is because you are in the state of yoga. You are experiencing yoga, you are practicing yoga, you are experiencing non-violence, you are practicing non-violence and you are non-violence. Shanti shanti shanti. We chant that because shanti is the value of non-violence, peace, be peace. Not be at peace, because to be at peace is to be in a fragile location. It is circumstantial and circumstances change and the peace is gone. The peace we are interested in is the peace with an unbreakable quality. It is not fragile. It cannot be broken. It is not a particular location bound by a certain theatrical setting. It is a peace that is unbounded. It requires no particular setting because you are it. You are peace. Shanti shanti shanti. Be peace, the state of peace, the practice of peace, the experience of peace. As you expand, you naturally drop your false, ego-made identities, the identities that create violence, the false identities that human beings are bound by.

The second yama is satya and it is an interesting one, because it is very dangerous to translate it merely as, "Thou shall speak the truth and truth only." The problem with truth is that everybody thinks they are speaking it. Of course, our truth is simply a reflection our state of consciousness. The reporter only reports from their state of consciousness. If that state of consciousness is conflicted, then what is perceived as occurring will be filtered through that conflict. Then the truth that one has access to is of no value and to simply translate satya as you should speak the truth is really of no use to us either. We must first explore what truth is. Is there really a truth that can be spoken? Thou shall speak the truth. Fanatics are willing to die for it, a truth which is actually an opinion. They start speaking it, shouting it, printing it, writing books about it, but it is only their belief that it is the truth. The truth that we are interested in belongs to no one, no individual, no collective, no ideology, no religion, no politician.

For something to be the truth, it has to be unchanging. For it to be unchanging, it has to be beyond time, beyond the consistent, persistent delusion of time. Anything that exists within time only has a relative value of truth. It is a truth only within a certain parameter, outside that parameter its value is no longer in the prism of truth. Not too long ago, you were allowed to smoke on a plane. It was true. I'm telling the truth. But it's not true anymore. Times have changed and so has the truth. The truth that Patanjali is talking about is the value of Self, the unchanging Sat, the essential nature of Self is Sat. Sat chit ananda. Sat meaning it has an absolute value. It is unchanging. From the yogic perspective, when we say it is unchanging, we mean it is beyond time. It is not fluctuating. So through the practice, experience and state of yoga, we can begin to have access to truth. This truth is not an ideology. This truth cannot be contained in a box. This truth cannot be put in a sentence or in ten commandments or any number of books, the Yoga Sutras included. Any works of literature, whether religious or scientific, none of them contain the total value of truth. They are mere attempts to explain a certain aspect of an infinite value, a truth for us now, but only from a certain viewpoint. So in its primary value, satya is the state of absoluteness, the unchanging consciousness. Sat chit ananda. It is eternal, before time. What is eternal? Eternal does not mean that it goes on forever. It means it is beyond the fluctuations of time because really, time is the greatest illusion there is. It is persistent and bewildering to the human mind, but it is an illusion nevertheless. At least the way we experience it in its linear progression is. As you continue the practice of yoga and begin to realize your own essential nature, a capacity starts to arise where you can know without knowing. You start to have access to the mind of god, to the unified field, or as the yogis call it, Hiranyagarbha, the unmanifested cosmic womb. In the Vedas it says, "Know that by knowing which everything else is known." That is Satya, to know That by knowing which everything else is known, because in that value all relative values of truth are contained. When we begin to experience that, then we start to have access to the multiple, relative values of truth.

What human beings call truth is far too highly rated. The whole world is lying but they all think they are speaking the truth. If we look at the linear history of humanity, we clearly see that what has made sense to human beings has been terrifying. The insane made sane. It has made sense because it has fitted within a certain spectrum of the truth, based on a particular viewpoint. To reduce satya to mean that you shall speak the truth is ridiculous because ultimately the truth cannot be spoken or written. The moment it is spoken or written, it becomes part of the relative reality. Even as you read this, right now, you bring your own understanding to it. The moment my words come off this page, their meaning belongs not to the writer, but to the reader. Each and every one of you who reads this has an absolute power, a total autonomy. You give meaning to what you read based on your own particular state of consciousness. If the experiencer is the experience, the writer is the written and the reader is the read, then how can one speak or write or read the truth? Really, it is not possible. That is the danger when one thinks that one can speak the absolute truth or write the absolute truth. That is when we have fanaticism. People die because of something written in a book thousands of years ago and taken at its literal value.

It would be ridiculous of us to think that Patanjali means that you should speak the truth. As your consciousness starts to open up to what is beyond the surface, you will start to have access to the infinite field, the field of silence, where there is no word, no ideology, no conditioning, no morality, no right or wrong, no judgement or fear. As you feel this greater and greater value of truth within your conscious mind, you begin to realize that truth belongs to no one, but you can belong to truth, to sat. As you start to belong to truth, to that field of silence, then your consciousness starts to open up. Your awareness starts to expand and as that awareness expands, you have access to more and more truth, more and more relative values of truth. Everything that exists in the relative world has a relative value of truth. As you start to have access to that, then you start to comprehend all the different points of view because now you are not bound by a certain position, your limited viewpoint. When somebody says, "There is no God," then that is true. When somebody else says, "Actually there is one God," that is true too. When somebody says, "There are many gods and goddesses," that is also true. When somebody says, "I am God," it's true. "God is only within." That is true. "God is dead." That is true too. They're all true to different people with different values, relative truths within a certain context, a certain parameter. But to hold on to any of these beliefs as the absolute value of truth, that is an act of violence. To try to hold on to any of that, to think that that is the absolute truth would be absurd. But the human nervous system has a tendency to reduce things, to hold on to things. If it is not refined, if it is not corrected, if it is not expanded, then it will limit, limit, limit its viewpoint because it is afraid. If a being is afraid and living in their isolated identity, how can they ever have access to the truth? They can access information, we have Google for that. But information is information. It's not truth, certainly not if it is on the internet.

Satya is not speaking the truth. Forget about speaking for once and enter the field of silence. Let truth speak to you. It speaks in silence. As you have greater and greater access to that silence, then you will have greater access to truth and you will begin to realize the relative value of all truth, spoken or written, heard or seen. Where one person sees one point of view, you will see ten, where someone else sees ten, you will see a hundred. At any moment, there are millions of possibilities and variables of the truth in existence. Layer upon layer upon layer. The more access you have to the absolute value of truth, then the more expansive will be the relative value of truth available to your consciousness. You are truthful to yourself, you are not lying to yourself anymore. Satya, the state of truth. The unchanging value of Self. Sat, pure consciousness. Silence. Why is it silent? Because it contains no vocabulary, no language. All our vocabulary, all our languages, are just our attempts to explain the silence, to explain the knowledge held in silence. The language of truth is silence. The greater the silence vibrating in you, the greater your access to the unchanging value of truth. This silence is full. This silence is brilliant. The most important practice is being truthful to yourself. Don't worry about speaking the truth to the world, because even if you speak the truth to the world, what they hear is up to them. You cannot control what people understand once you have uttered something. Words cannot contain truth.

The third yama is asteya, meaning non-stealing. Now again, as with the previous two yamas, the meaning of asteya is not limited to just non-stealing. That would be quite humorous, "Hey, don't steal." "Yes, got it!" Of course, we don't steal.

So we have to really explore asteya, the first meaning of which is, when you are in the state of yoga, you start to become non-attached. Natural detachment starts to arise. Do you remember how you came here into this reality, naked and with nothing? And when the last breath moves through this body, everything that one thinks one owns will stay here. What will go with you is your state of consciousness. Asteya is the realization that nothing is owned by you. No one actually owns anything. This idea of me, of mine, drops away. Yes, you might use these words to help convey the meaning for those who don't really understand, when it is relevant, but this idea of ownership will drop away. This detachment does not mean there is no care. There is a lot of care, love and attention in you, but these ideas of ownership of anything will fade because this idea of I own this or that is ridiculous. You don't own anything. Nobody owns anything. So in the state of yoga, there is a natural letting go, a detachment. You surrender.

You see, these yamas all fit together. You cannot practice one without the other. The hunger of the mind knows no end. We all understand the truth of this. But through the yogic practice you can begin to transcend the lower mind and so naturally asteya starts to happen. As long as you are within the mind, the mind will constantly be looking for something else. It is constantly bound by what it has and what it does not have, who it is and who it is yet to be. It is constantly struggling to attain something it doesn't have or be something it is not. But through the great art of letting go, you receive totality. Ultimately, the totality is you. You belong to totality and totality belongs to you.

Asteya is that natural letting go, the natural detachment, transcending the lower mind value which is constantly dissatisfied, in a constant state of dissatisfaction with life. A life which has been given to us to live and enjoy and yet, the mind encounters this life with a great resistance. The individual finds life unbearable and experiences life as an existential burden. When one is in this state, one can enter any space and take from it, with a mind that is constantly taking, taking, taking. We have all met people like this, energy vampires in a dense state of consciousness. No matter what space they enter, they suck the energy, the very life force from it. As you move toward a greater state of unity, a state of yoga, no matter what space you enter you will always fill it with your light. You will add to the space wherever you go. You will naturally pour more energy into the environment because you will have access to the infinite value. As you have access to this infinite value, this unity consciousness, you will naturally be giving out more because you will now be receiving from the source value and the more you give, the more you will receive. You will not be trying to give, but it will naturally become who you are. It will just become your natural nature. That is the true value of asteya and as you practice it, you will see, wherever you are in life, you are adding to the space. Asteya.

The state of asteya, the practice of asteya and the experience of asteya. This experience is what? More and more abundance. Greater and greater fulfilment. As you are fulfilled, you will no longer have an endlessly hungry mind. That does not mean to say that you will not have desire. Desire will still come, but now that desire will be more in alignment with nature. It will be evolutionary desire, desire moving through you, not bound to you. It will be celebratory, magnificent, brilliant. This is not a puritanical teaching. That is not what Patanjali is about, that you must become a nun, live like a monk or suppress yourself and hope for the best. This practice will add to the value of bliss, to the value of life. Asteya is not about not having. It is a state of consciousness where this whole idea of having and not having drops away. When that idea drops, then you realize you are in the state of yoga, in totality. Totality has become available to you. In that totality, the having or not having function of totality is no longer causing any stress because it is a state of abundance, of true prosperity, a state of celebration.

The fourth one is brahmacharya, often translated as celibacy. Now that right there is a recipe for schizophrenia. If you study yoga, you will see it is a celebration of energy. One of the primary symbols of the Hindu yogic tradition is the Shiva lingam, the phallic symbol. The lingam and the yoni merged together, the male symbol with the female symbol. So to say that Patanjali is advising the yogi to be celibate is ridiculous. I don't know where these ideas originate. Brahmacharya, two words come together to make this word: brahma, cosmic Self and acharya, the one who is devoted to That, speaking as That, seeing as That, teaching as That, being That. When the yogi is in a state of unity then they are a brahmachari, meaning they are radiating the value of brahma. Wherever they go, whatever they do, they are experiencing brahma, totality. If you are looking at a rose and you are experiencing the full value of the rose that is brahmacharya. You are experiencing the brahma. Experiencing the whole rose. Or the whole apple. Or another individual. In the yogic tradition, there is no shunning of any energetic expressions which are natural to human beings. So brahmacharya here is the state of consciousness where you start to experience things based on their fullest value. When you look at a flower, you are no longer labelling that flower as merely a rose. Now you are able to experience the full value of that intelligence.

A brahamachari is the practitioner of brahmacharya and is devoted, has surrendered absolutely to the realization of Self, to the expansion of consciousness and of course, everything that comes with it. You no longer give up the diamond for the banana, because you are a brahmachari. You are progressing in that expansive state of consciousness and you are experiencing the universe, experiencing the love affair between you and the universe. When you are in that state, then naturally the energy will not dissipate.

The confusion about brahmacharya meaning celibacy came about because people naturally had sexual desires but were unable to define this desire, so they either suppressed it which caused all kinds of psychosis, or they obsessed about it, which again caused all kinds of psychosis. Or when they were having sexual interaction, they were depleted by that experience so they assumed that the suppression of sexuality was what brahmacharya meant. But that is not what yoga is about. Yoga is not about suppression or obsession, it is about transformation. As you go into the truest value of any energy, you transform it because all energy is essentially arising from pure consciousness. Shiva, Shakti, Shiva, Shakti, Shiva, Shakti. Brahmacharya is the play of Shiva, Shakti, not the suppression of Shiva, Shakti. It is the religious interpretation of brahmacharya that says one should be celibate. It's a joke. Brahmacharya is not celibacy. Patanjali would not be so ridiculous. Otherwise your desire would lead you to a state of weakness. The energy arising would be forcing you here and there, your desire would be taking you here and there. When you are in the state of brahmacharya, everything is meditative. When you are eating, it is meditative. When you are walking, it is meditative. When you are laughing, it is meditative. If you are with another person in an intimate manner, it is meditative. All of it is meditative. Try it, the next time you see a rose, take a moment. You will realize that in that flower is the totality of what Is, because that flower is an expression of infinite intelligence. The lower mind can label it and say, "Oh, I know this flower, it's a rose." But there is no actual rose sitting there thinking, "I'm a rose." The word rose is something we have invented to define a certain intelligence, which shows up in a certain manner and we call it a rose. What if you drop that name and you really encounter this being, whom we call rose? The word will disappear. Brahmacharya. That is the brahmacharya we are interested in. That is the brahmacharya that is relevant for us. Not this strange puritanical religious interpretation of it.

Aparigraha is the last yama and is similar to asteya. Aparigraha meaning to be without possessions, dropping the idea of possession. Asteya and aparigraha are very similar in their meaning. If you are established in one, the other will naturally be experienced. Again, sometimes people misunderstand it as not owning anything. They take it to mean that one has to live in very strange conditions, without possessions. This is not what aparigraha is about.

Aparigraha is not about punishing yourself. It is about accessing the state of consciousness where the needs drop, being in a state of non-neediness. You are no longer needy. When you are not in the state of neediness or dependency, then your desires will be natural desires. If it is nature's will that you have to sleep on the cold floor, then you will do that and you will have a beautiful experience. If it is nature's will that you sleep in the bed, you will have a wonderful experience in the bed. If it is nature's will that you walk barefoot for miles, then you will walk barefoot for miles and that too, will be wonderful. Aparigraha. Infinite adaptability. As you go deeper into the state of yoga, you will develop this infinite adaptability, an infinite capacity to deal with what life is asking of you. That is the mastery of life. You are able to arrive at whatever is required, whatever the universe is asking of you. This is the state of aparigraha. Yes, for those who are in a denser state of consciousness, aparigraha is decluttering, getting rid of stuff, simplifying our life. We are, after all, merely temporary custodians of all this stuff we fill our lives with.

These yamas: ahimsa, satya, asteya, brahmacharya, aparigraha, are not there to make you feel bad about yourself. That is never the purpose of yogic teachings. These are not moral codes. Morality makes you feel burdened. These yamas are there to help you evolve and transcend.

जातिदेशकालसमयानवच्छिन्नाः
सार्वभौमा महाव्रतम् ॥ ३१ ॥

2:31 Jati desha kala samaya anavachchhinnah sarvabhauma mahavratam

The practice of yoga has to be invoked irrespective of the circumstances or situation. No matter where you are, the moment you invoke the practice, if you practice totally, you will find yourself liberated. Regardless of what is going on on the surface value, if you pour yourself fully, honestly and truthfully, and with absolute sincerity, into the practice, you will find yourself rise up. You will find yourself expand. You will find yourself transcend.

There is no moment in time, no circumstance, when the practice is not of value because the true practice of yoga is holistic, it is all encompassing. It will merge all aspects of life. As I have discussed, the biggest scripture about yoga, the Bhagavad Gita, explains how the practice of yoga is relevant even on the battlefield. No matter what situation you are in, no matter what justification the mind is giving itself to go on its loop of insanity, know that the practice is right, the practice is relevant. Pour yourself into it and see the magic happen. When you transcend, that is how you gain authentic power and a sense of serenity. You are no longer afraid of yourself because ultimately, all the fear one harbors within one's psyche is a fear of oneself, one's own capability to cope with life, or not. When you begin to discover the eternal flow of power within your Being, you discover you are fearless because you are infinitely capable. That is not an arrogant idea. That idea comes with a deep sense of humility, a deep sense of surrender.

शौचसंतोषतपःस्वाध्यायेश्वरप्रणिधानानि
नियमाः ॥ ३२ ॥

2:32 Saucha santosha tapah svadhyaya ishvara pranidhanani niyamah

Patanjali introduces us to the five niyamas, the first one being saucha. There are, of course, multiple levels of meaning that arise from saucha, but the word literally means purity. Not purity in a puritanical sense, but purity meaning to not hold toxins within, on either a physical or a psychological level. Patanjali explains that the practice of saucha and the experience of saucha are crucial for one's progress in the state of yoga. On a purely physical level of course, he is very clear that we should keep the physical body free of toxins. It's a very obvious thing, but somehow human beings find it very difficult. We find it very challenging and are constantly putting toxins in our body. Yet we pride ourselves on having incredible intellect and intelligence, the most advanced species on this planet. However, no other species markets its toxins as food, plastic as food, chemicals as food, food which has nothing to do with nature, but is purely produced in factories. So the primary meaning of saucha is the practice of not putting toxins in our body or in the body of the universe. Saucha meaning not being of a toxic influence, not consuming toxins, not eating refined, packaged foods, eating mindfully, eating more and more fresh, farm-to-table, locally sourced, seasonal produce, full of prana. It's really not that difficult to not consume food that has traces of violence in it. We need to consume mindfully and be alert to what we are putting into the environment. It does not work if you are mindful of consuming more consciously, while you are not alert to what we are putting out into nature. It has to be a two-way process, not consuming toxins and not putting toxins out into nature.

On the subtler level, saucha is the practice of cleansing and releasing the patterns within the body. Our body has bio-memory, so the practice of kriyas found in the tantric tradition, the use of mantras and certain breathwork, certain asanas, all help us to release the biochemical toxins that the body holds on to, the toxic memory. On a cellular level, this bio-memory that the body carries, this toxic memory, is not just contained within the mind, it permeates throughout the whole body, every cell is a packet of information, toxic information. The practice of saucha on that subtler level, is the use of these techniques to release all the toxins, the bio-memory, being held in the body, while at the same time releasing the information which is not serving one's evolution. That is where the kriya work and the pranayama practice are especially relevant.

On another level, the saucha practice is to relieve the mind of toxic patterns, thoughts, belief systems, identities, to release these toxic relationships we carry through our lives. It is quite fascinating how deeply human beings are addicted to self-destructive behavior, addicted to suffering, to creating suffering for themselves and suffering for their fellow beings. On the subtlest level, saucha is the release of the toxic thought patterns. We now can identify them and open up to release them. Then the essential quality of our brilliance can shine forth. This process of releasing the toxicity in ourselves may also involve letting go of the toxic relations in our lives, releasing all holding patterns. A yogi is not holding on to anything anymore. There is no codependency. That is the practice of saucha.

Some translations suggest saucha is merely about cleanliness, that one should take a bath. I think to attribute that meaning to Patanjali would be quite comical, that this guy imparts all this incredible knowledge and then says, "Hey, don't forget to take a shower." I think that your mother would have said that enough times when you were a kid. It's okay if you forget to take a shower, you can still practice saucha. Patanjali is not going to be mad at you.

The second niyama Patanjali addresses is santosha. Santosha is the experience of grace. A deep state of equanimity. Sometimes the word contentment is used to describe santosha, but contentment can be misunderstood. People often think of contentment as a compromise, to be satisfied, to be okay with what you have. That is really not what santosha means. Yes, maybe at the densest level of its understanding, santosha can mean that, but it is actually the experience of, the practice of and the state of a deep awareness of grace that is your life, in any moment, irrespective of what you have and what you don't have. If somebody asked you to make a list of everything you have received, experienced and enjoyed in this life, I think it would take you a very long time to complete that list. So obviously santosha is not referring to being happy with your lot. It is about experiencing grace, irrespective of what you do or don't have. The experience of grace has nothing to do with whether you do or don't have possessions. Here, santosha is referring to that stage in the practice where you begin to acknowledge the grace that is present in your life at all times.

As the yogi begins to experience deep santosha, which can also be translated as equanimity, they will become non-resistant, start to resist nothing. Whatever is arising in the moment, they will have no resistance to because they have become equanimous with what Is. As you drop all resistance, you discover what lies beneath the surface value is the eternal flow of grace, the mystery of grace. I call it the mystery of grace, because it cannot be reduced by the analytical mind. It mysteriously flows eternally, without any particular effort, yet it touches every being. This practice of equanimity is the dropping of all resistance to what Is, the letting go of this whole story about what you have, what you don't have, who you are, what you would rather be and the chasm in between being filled with conflict. As you allow this equanimity to rise, you start to acknowledge the bit that is your life in every breath you take. A deep state of appreciation in what Is then starts to rise and in that state of appreciation, you are naturally filled with energy, vitality. Your mind naturally becomes clearer and you can then act in alignment with the natural law rather than against it. You are no longer in an ungrateful state, constantly complaining. No matter who you are in this world of seven billion and counting human creatures, if you were asked to list three things you don't like about your life, I don't think anybody would have difficulty in coming up with those three things, no matter who they are, because if you ask the mind to go looking, then it will find something to complain about. That is the nature of the lower mind, to be in a state of conflict with what Is, and that is not going to serve anyone on their spiritual journey. For wherever they are, something will always be missing. They may arrive at a new location and it will be charming for a while. Then the mind will normalize it, it will become familiar. The moment the mind becomes familiar with it, it will take it for granted and look for something else, something new, something that could have been, should have been and so on and so forth. And that is a sure way to hell.

We are not discussing insane behavior here. We are talking about equanimity and a state of consciousness that is incredibly intelligent, a subtler level of intelligence, where you have access to a state of consciousness within you which is not a fragile one, not dependent on a particular set of circumstances. The weak individual, who does not have access to this subtler level, will be affected by every little fluctuation in the surface value and often go into a state of crisis. For most human beings that seems to be the story of their life, a state of crisis. So santosha is that state where there is no crisis. Yes, there are difficulties. Troubling experiences will still occur, but when you have equanimity, you are not affected by them and so you can find the state, the presence of grace irrespective of what is happening on the surface value. You can connect to the cosmic value that is santosha. You are filled with ease, an ease in your being, and from that place right action will arise, appropriate action. Santosha, equanimity.

Patanjali has put these niyamas together so beautifully. First is saucha, where the practitioner naturally gains a clarity of perception. The nervous system is not stressed and so it has much more access to the state of equanimity. Santosha can contain an inner calm, an inner peace, irrespective of what is going on on the surface value. Then when the nervous system can have access to a greater amount of inner peace, it is naturally filled with passion, the third niyama is tapah, an optimal amount of energy.

Tapah as a word means fire. So on one level, tapah means the yogi is filled with an intensity, filled with a passion. It is very important for us to realize that these ritual teachings of the yog-vedantic tradition are not suggesting you become some kind of a flat-lining being, going into some spiritually vegetative state, denying the world. No. The yogi cultivates a life filled with passion and approaches their practice with that level of passion, that level of presence. You will discover when you begin to approach life with that passion and the state of presence, that a certain level of optimal energy will become available to you. You will gain a greater sense of flow in every aspect of your life. Tapah is this radical quality of presence, no more half-assing through life. Whatever you are engaged in, you are engaged in it with the totality of your being. This half-assed approach to life, so popular among human beings, is toxic; it makes nature scream in agony. You have to cultivate this capacity of tapah so that no matter what is going on in your life, when you arrive at anything, you arrive with a fullness, with a vitality. Whatever you engage in, you do it with totality, you make it a sacred act. You will find when you cultivate this practice in your life, that you will have a greater and greater experience of yoga, of unity consciousness. You will begin to realize that when you are in that state, when you are absolutely engaged, you will have access to a level of intelligence which you wouldn't usually have. When the separation between the moment and the observer disappears, when they merge, you will have access to a level of intelligence which is very refined.

Another meaning of tapah is self-mastery, of watching oneself, mindful of not cultivating any level of dependency. For example, you might find you have become dependent on technology or on a certain food or caffeine, so the practice would be to give up certain things for a certain duration of time. But at the same time, tapah is also when you take up a certain set of practices or techniques, with a particular intention for a particular duration of time. Let's say you chose to do a certain amount of repetitions of a particular mantra, with a specific intention for a week and you complete it. You then get a sense of self-mastery. It's a great practice to bring into your life.

Tapah is also when we go on pilgrimages, when we step out of our comfort zone, challenge ourselves. We are wild beings that have actually been domesticated in these times. It's a huge accident, so there is still this great need in us to expand and have adventure. Tapah, on that level, is the practice of pushing the envelope, putting you out of your comfort zone, cultivating tapah in your life because if you stay within your bubble, your bubble will, after a while, consume you. I always say, get comfortable but not too comfortable or else you become comfortably numb. That's tapah, passion, self-mastery and self-transcendence.

The fourth niyama is svadhyaya. Patanjali has mentioned svadhyaya before, the studying of oneself, observing oneself. As one goes deeper within one's essential nature, a natural self-observation arises, an observation without judgement, which is a deep aspect of the state of yoga, the practice of yoga and the experience of yoga. The other meaning of svadhyaya is self-practice when nobody is watching, when there is no external validation to be had. Being able to devote yourself to a certain level of practice, to a certain level of awareness, when there is no external validation to be had, is going to be the most effective. Svadhyaya, the studying of oneself and studying through oneself.

The fifth niyama is ishvara pranidhanani, surrender, the absolute state of surrender. To continue the state of surrender, the practice of surrender and the experience of surrender. Devotion, humility and surrender to the Divine that is held in your heart, without which life would be very dry. Practice it, this deep surrender, and experience it. Let go of this idea that the universe is hostile. There is only love. That is all that is happening. Devotional surrender is key, being pulled by the spirit. Don't resist it. Cultivate this love affair.

वितर्कबाधने प्रतिपक्षभावनम् ॥ ३३ ॥

2:33 Vitarkabadhane pratipakshabhavanam

The tendencies which arise within the field of our consciousness, which run contrary to the niyamas and the yamas, have to be examined through the light of awareness and through that examination they will naturally fall away. For example, if you start to complain about your life, then examine that action. No matter how logical the reasoning behind your complaint is, if you want to experience the state of yoga, you must examine it fully and you will realize that it is totally contrary to the niyama, santosha. As you examine that through the lens of santosha, you will drop it. As you drop it, you will then find yourself in appreciation of your life. And in that appreciation, you will discover a great power which will help you make your life better. Why? Because the experiencer is the experience. Your particular life does not exist outside your consciousness. How do you know that? Because when you die, life itself goes on, only you are not here. That's all. Everything that happens in your life is in the field of your consciousness. As you correct your consciousness, so your life corrects itself. It is a great tool. Establish yourself in the understanding of yoga. When you find yourself at times uncertain, terrified by life, use your tools, bring ishvara pranidhanani into your consciousness, deep surrender. Use the intelligence that is you, that is the totality of existence, and realize the absolute absurdity of worrying about what might be. Surrender to that grace and you will find yourself filled with courage, filled with love. The fear might still be there but now you will move the way love makes you move.

वितर्का हिंसादयः कृतकारितानुमोदिता

लोभक्रोधमोहपूर्वका मृदुमध्याधिमात्रा दुः

खाज्ञानानन्तफला इति प्रतिपक्षभावनम् ॥ ३४ ॥

2:34 Vitarkaa hinsadayah krita karita anumodita lobha krodha moha purvakah mridu madhya adhimatra duhkha ajnana anantafalah iti pratipakshabhavanam

Here Patanjali says that ultimately all violence that arises in one's being, whether directed at oneself or at others, arises from incorrect knowledge. As true knowledge, correct knowledge, starts to dawn within and one connects with this pure field of knowledge, one finds that naturally there is spontaneous right action, more and more dharma, less and less karma. Karma is the action arising ultimately from a state of conflict with nature. Dharma is in alignment with the law of nature.

That doesn't mean to say that it is not unpleasant to go through certain stuff, but one thing is for sure. It ultimately leads one to evolution, to an expansion of consciousness, expansion of being, and a greater state within one's own heart.

अहिंसाप्रतिष्ठायां तत्सन्निधौ वैरत्यागः ॥ ३५ ॥

2:35 Ahimsa pratishthayam tat samnidhau vaira tyagah

From sutras 35 to 45, Patanjali discusses the siddhis, the great benefits, powers, and blessings that one starts to experience within one's being as one moves deeper and deeper into the state of yoga, within the context of the yamas and niyamas. Here he discusses the fact that the experiencer is the experience, the observer is the observed, the dancer is the dance, and as the experiencer starts to alter and change, then invariably the way that he or she experiences the world will also start to change. The external reality will appear to change too, because the fact is the universe likes to organize itself around the most consistent frequency you hold, whatever that consistent frequency may be. That is not to say that every aspect of oneself within that dimension will adhere to that vibrational frequency, but it is a fairly safe bet that within a certain proximity, the universe that is experienced in the external realm to one's body will start to reflect the same value as that being experienced within, ahimsa pratishthayam tat samnidhau vaira tyagah.

As we've said before, ahimsa, the first of the yamas, is non-violence. Pratishthayam is the firmly established state, vaira is hostility and tyagah is abandonment. As ever, there are several meanings here. One is to be moving in the direction of and the other is getting established in, the state of ahimsa. When Patanjali says established in the state of ahimsa, he is not speaking merely of a static location of one's consciousness, for one cannot as far as their individual expression goes, maintain a certain state within a static context. It has to be dynamic. As we have said before, it is the state, the practice and the experience of yoga. So as one gets more and more established in ahimsa, truly begins to experience ahimsa, then within the proximity of the yogi all hostility is abandoned. Within their vicinity, all violence starts to be dissolved. The experiencer is the experience and as their experience is no longer of violence, then their presence naturally starts to emanate the value of peace. This in turn has the potential of disarming anybody they come into contact with. Now here, it is very important for us to realize it does not just mean physical proximity. There can be an individual within the physical proximity of a great master, but if that individual is not receptive, they will not be able to receive that value of peace.

Patanjali is talking about the yogi's experience of the external realm and the impact that the yogi's vibration can have on the environment around them, including the proximity to the soul. When the yogi is established in the great value of love and non-violence, they will find that all hostility around them drops away. Anybody who comes within close proximity to that yogi, on a physical level and also the subtler level of the soul, will also gain in the great value of peace, the great value of love, simply by being close to that yogi. And that is how we change the world. As more and more people are established in the state of ahimsa, the environment around them starts to have greater and greater value of ahimsa. As more and more people move toward this value, then we have a world which is dominated by the value of ahimsa. As in the story of Angulimala and the Buddha. When the ruthless bandit, Angulimala, approaches Buddha, instead of ferociously cutting off his finger, a window of opportunity opens up to him because Buddha is established in the state, the practice and the experience of ahimsa. The non-violent Buddha provides the violent Angulimala with the chance to drop his violence, his trauma, his narrative he uses to justify the violence he impacts on other people. It opens up a window where he can drop that violence and the transformation can become available to him. It's a wonderful example of how when within close proximity to such a Being, hostility simply drops away. For to have hostility toward someone, anyone, means to have distance from them, to have distance in one's heart, to shut off one's heart to them. That is not yoga.

सत्यप्रतिष्ठायां क्रियाफलाश्रयत्वम् ॥ ३६ ॥

2:36 Satya pratishthayam kriyafalashrayatvam

As the yogi becomes established in satya, starts to experience satya, then they start to have access to the absolute value of truth, the unchanging value of truth. As one starts to have greater and greater access to that, to be established in that knowledge, then naturally one's actions and words start to have the value of kriya, of evolutionary action. One develops the incredible power found in words and actions for manifestation. Why? Because all that one perceives that is manifested, the invisible manifesting in the visible dimension, is the Absolute. When one starts to consistently have access to that dimension of reality, to the dimension of satya, then naturally one starts to have access to kriyafala and so be able to generate much that one can enjoy.

There is great joy in eating the fruits of our labors. There is not a lot of joy in working hard and there being no fruit to reward us. We want the fruit. But we find that people are working and nothing happens and nothing happens and nothing happens. So they think, "What is wrong, what am I doing wrong?" People always assume that there is something wrong if they are not getting what they want, then they start to doubt themselves. "Am I doing the right thing?" They doubt the universe. "Is god angry with me? Why me, Lord, why? I have been doing everything correctly. What am I doing wrong?" This kind of asshole behavior is not satya. As one becomes established in satya, then invariably one's experiences of satya, one's experience of fulfilment, a consistent state of fulfilment, is maintained. The state of supreme bliss is maintained and that then gives us the power of manifestation. Our words can manifest, our actions bear fruit. But it's dynamic, not static. Some individuals may think, "I'm not established in satya because I did this thing and I didn't get a result." But if that occurs, then you drop that action. That is the result. Drop that action and focus your energy somewhere else. In the state of satya, you don't have a certain rigidity within yourself, an obsessive nature. People, when it comes to manifestation, can become obsessive and in that obsessiveness they can miss the point. In satya the fruit comes from the kriya, not karma, because if the karma is heavy and dense then you keep experiencing your karma. But when you go deeper and deeper into the state of yoga, establishing yourself in unity consciousness and having access to satya, you are filled with bliss. So naturally your external realm also radiates that and you will find your life getting more and more abundant. In that state, it has to happen. Now if you have incorrect intellect of what abundance means, then you are not in satya. It's a clear sign.

Any complaint is a clear sign that you are not in satya, you are in ignorance. Any complaint that arises within you and you believe in it, that's a clear sign that you're not in satya. The "but why me" behavior is a clear sign that you've got your head up your butt. A lot of people are like this, legs up on the table, typing on their brand new Mac about all the problems they have, how they're not able to manifest enough. That's poverty consciousness, that's not satya.

As you move deeper into satya, then naturally your experience has to be blissful and your power to manifest will naturally increase, it has to increase. But it only increases when you have the capacity to perceive your manifestation. Words start to have that power. Many times my master would say, "Oh, this is what is going to happen" and it would happen. That is why we value the word of the yogi so much. It's not about idolizing an individual. It is idolizing the voice of truth. That voice arising from a greater value of the Absolute is the Absolute speaking, no other. Only thyself and the Absolute is speaking. Then we just listen and when we learn to listen to the voice of the Absolute, then we have a greater and greater capacity to speak the Absolute. You cannot speak the Absolute if you don't listen to the Absolute. Satya pratishthayam kriyafalashrayatvam. How beautiful is that? On becoming established in the state of satya, we find our life starts to have that value. Our actions take on the value of kriya and we enjoy the fruits of our kriya. It is most important that we enjoy the fruit.

अस्तेयप्रतिष्ठायां सर्वरत्नोपस्थानम् ॥ ३७॥

2:37 Asteyapratishthayam sarvaratnopasthanam

As we have discussed in sutra 30 of pada 2, as one experiences the state of asteya, all the gems start to present themselves to the individual. Ratna, gems, sarvaratnopasthanam, all the gems. The more the person chases the less they have. So the way to prosperity is not by chasing it. It is by raising one's deserving power. Only then will all the gems present themselves to that individual. Life becomes full of jewels. All the jewels, all the gems, will reveal themselves to the individual. The jewels of life and natural prosperity will come to the individual moving in the direction of asteya, the state, the practice and the experience of asteya. One then starts to experience abundance, the jewels of life. One starts to gain a natural capacity to appreciate what Is, appreciate all the gems that are here.

Patanjali is saying that all the gems are presenting themselves all the time. When you experience asteya, you develop the capacity to perceive these gems that are always presenting, because the being who is not refining themselves and is in a state of disharmony within themselves, a state of stress, is not able to perceive the gems.

They just don't have the capacity. But the being who is moving in the direction of asteya is able to perceive the gems of life. As you develop your perception of them, the jewels of life present themselves to you more and more and more.

In the higher states of consciousness, this dimension of reality becomes heaven. These are all descriptions of heaven. It is not off in a cloud, not in some distant other, but in the here and the now. In asteya, all the gems come to you. There is no lack in any aspect of your life. For there to be lack, one has to be bound by ignorance within oneself. For one to experience lack within oneself, one has to be living in a very hostile universe. "I want this, I'm not getting it. I did it right, but I'm not getting it. Who is not giving it to me?" You're living in a very hostile universe. You did the work. You planted the seed, but the tree is not growing. Why is it not growing? That must mean you are in a very hostile universe, but the universe is you, so where are you living? You are living in hostility within yourself; all hostility is directed toward self. What a beautiful sutra this is. As you become established in asteya, all the gems come to you. All the beauty of life reveals itself to you and more and more comes because beauty attracts beauty.

ब्रह्मचर्यप्रतिष्ठायां वीर्यलाभः ॥ ३८ ॥

2:38 Brahmacharya pratishthayam viryalabhah

Virya is vitality and abhah is gain. So as one moves into brahmacharya, which we have explored at length in the yamas, as one gets established in it, moves in that direction, into that state, a great vitality is experienced and one is full of energy. We are able to transmute the energy. Instead of energy consumption, we learn the art of transmuting the energy, so great courage and vitality fills the individual. One of the siddhis is this gain, this tangible experience. These are all tangible experiences, gems coming to us, this power of manifestation, all hostility being dropped. You go somewhere where the doors have been shut and now the doors open to you. You have experienced that in your own life. When you are in that particular state, when you are in the state of flow, doors open for you. These are all tangible experiences Patanjali is discussing, which make life more and more charming for us.

अपरिग्रहस्थैर्ये जन्मकथंतासंबोधः ॥ ३९ ॥

2:39 Aparigraha sthairye janmakathanta sanbodhah

Through becoming established in aparigraha, Patanjali says, non-local knowledge starts to become available to us, knowledge about our different lifetimes becomes available to us, supreme knowledge naturally starts to come. Now this knowledge is not just about words. Having access to non-local knowledge means that you're having access to knowledge which is intuitive, knowledge which is very clear. It's a certain intuition; there is no doubt, no shakiness in this knowledge. A complete, conclusive knowledge starts to arise in you that is not linear, just conclusive, a knowing. It's like a whole knowledge downloading in you, then you discover that you know things beyond your memory.

शौचात् स्वाङ्गजुगुप्सा परैरसंसर्गः ॥ ४० ॥

2:40 Sauchat svanggajugupsa parairasansargah

As one practices saucha, goes deeper into the state of saucha, one starts to naturally transcend body attachment. A clear body is a light body and no longer holds you down. As we have discussed in sutra 32 of pada 2, through the practice of saucha, by releasing the toxins and becoming more established in saucha, one starts to naturally transcend body attachment and one's fundamental identity as merely being the body. One can celebrate the body as it becomes a portal into infinity. Every experience of the body is experienced by the supreme Being; the supreme Being enjoys itself through the body. Every cosmic experience starts to be enjoyed through the physiology.

It is a great act of self-hatred that has been sold in the marketplace of religion, that anything that the body enjoys is wrong. It is a ridiculous concept that any experience that can be experienced by the body should be considered wrong, it's a very strange thing. Through the practice of saucha, one naturally starts to transcend the body attachment. So the more we refine the body, the more we are able to transcend our identity primarily as the body. As this happens, naturally the body becomes more and more filled with cosmic intelligence. The supreme Being acquires this body, this nervous system; the supreme Being acquires this mouth, acquires these eyes, acquires this nose, acquires this tongue, acquires this skin. The supreme Being, the cosmic creative intelligence, acquires this whole physiology and then this experience which is being experienced through this body has a cosmic value. It explodes like a supernova effect, because the supreme Being is enjoying it now. A cosmic experience starts to occur. Naturally, craving is no longer there. One starts to develop non-attachment, vairagyam, and there is a greater ecstasy.

Put a knife in the water and it will absorb the blade. You take the knife out and it leaves no impression. If you stick the same knife in a wooden table, the surface will resist the blade. You have to stab it hard to get it into the wood and when you pull the knife out, the mark will remain and everyone who sees it will know it was stabbed by a knife. This is like a rigid consciousness, a dense consciousness. A greater, illuminated consciousness, like the water, will not resist and no impression is left. A great depth of experience is absorbed, but there is no impression, no scarring; it is without any attachment. This is how cosmic experience is, how cosmic bliss is experienced. Dense bliss leaves a hatred of the body, craving, shame, guilt. Anything the body wants, it gets and this creates the problem of perpetual craving, aversion, craving, aversion, craving, aversion. But from the bliss state, natural detachment starts to be experienced. One becomes indifferent toward one's body. That does not mean one hates one's body. One starts to transcend it, one does not get obsessed about one's body. A body that has been put through saucha creates a mind which is not obsessed with its body, always standing in front of the mirror looking at itself. People spend a lot of time in front of the mirror. It's their secret, standing in front of the mirror hating themselves, always wishing they could have something else. If they could only get the body they wanted, everything would be all right. But if they do get it, they panic that they cannot maintain it. "What will happen if I don't look like this?" What will happen to their instagram followers? People become more and more body-obsessed and doing extreme yoga postures. That's not yoga. It is not the idea of yoga to sculpt the body. It is to transcend body consciousness and one's identity of primarily being the body.

When your body is acquired by cosmic intelligence, every experience of that body now has cosmic value. Whether you are having a coffee, taking a walk, dipping in the Ganga or hugging somebody, the experience is cosmic. When the cosmos is hugging, it's a cosmic hug. If your nervous system is not acquired by the cosmos, how can you have a cosmic hug? You can fantasize about a cosmic hug, but you cannot experience it. It's like a thought experiment. If there was a person who studied and studied apples, but had never eaten one and then one day they finally ate one, did they learn anything new? Of course they did. It's very clear that all that study can be nullified by a moment of verified experience. You cannot explain the universe just within the context of theories, which is what western science tries to do. You must experience cosmic unity to understand it. You cannot explain the apple just by talking about the apple. That's what the yogis have always known. Here we're being given the technology to experience it, so we have the theoretical knowledge, but we also have the experience within ourselves. Just as somebody who eats the apple and who knows the story of the apple has a deeper knowledge than someone who only reads about it.

सत्त्वशुद्धिसौमनस्यैकाग्र्येन्द्रिय
जयात्मदर्शनयोग्यत्वानि च ॥ ४१ ॥

2:41 Sattvashuddhi saumanasyaikagryen driyajayatmada rshana yojnatvani cha

Patanjali now discusses the subtler value of saucha. As one goes deeper into saucha, one develops a cheerfulness. A greater capacity for cheerfulness within oneself is gained through the practice of saucha. This is something we should always practice. Some people when they wake up in the morning act as if they've been beaten up all night. They just wake up angry, already upset with life. You can see it in their face, that's their default state. Ikagrya, the capacity to be focused, have one-pointedness, is very important because without that we cannot be relevant. A person who does not have that capacity cannot be relevant.

As we start to clear away that which is no longer relevant to us and go deeper into our practice, releasing that which is not our true Self, releasing the toxicity, we start to gain the vision of sattva. As we gain the vision of sattva within ourself, cheerfulness starts to develop. The capacity to be in the state of cheerfulness, genuine cheerfulness, not a fake cheerfulness, starts to become available to us, this one-pointedness. The mind starts to be purified and gain greater value of the soul, greater value of the Absolute. The mind becomes cheerful, the mind becomes focused. The senses become more refined and within our consciousness, they become more supportive of evolution. Then our senses are able to draw in a lot more information, but at the same time they don't go where we don't want them to go. Otherwise, you find that even if you don't want to focus on something, your mind will go there. It is like a teenager with a pimple on their face, obsessed with it when they look in the mirror, that's all they see, their imperfection. So when our senses come within the field of our soul, the cosmos starts to reveal itself to us and then we start to have access to the saumanasya, to the hidden value in every finite expression. The self is seen and witnessed and experienced.

संतोषाद् अनुत्तमः   सुखलाभः ॥ ४२ ॥

2:42 Santoshad anuttamah sukhalabhah

Through santosha one experiences supreme bliss, unexcelled bliss, a bliss which cannot be topped. Without santosha there is no bliss, Patanjali says. Only through the state, the practice and the experience of santosha can one gain an unexcelled happiness. Only through santosha can one enjoy great ecstasy, great joy. Santosha, as discussed in sutra 32 of book 2, is contentment that continues to move in the direction of more. Not contentment as in negation, because the universe does not support sameness, the universe supports more. The universe is always moving in the direction of more. But if a mind is not established in the absoluteness, then its perpetual movement in the direction of more is violent. It is filled with lack, conflict, restlessness and misery. Nothing is ever enough. However, if a mind is established in santosha, then its movement in the direction of more is backed by bliss and gratefulness. As you go deeper and deeper into your illuminated consciousness, you naturally get greater and greater contentment, greater and greater bliss and more and more creativity surrounds you. You become busier and busier without feeling busy. Enlightenment is a very busy state from the point of view of a dense mind, but from the point of view of the illuminated mind it is not busyness. It is simply what is happening to you. You are just becoming more and more cosmic within yourself. The cosmos is busy all the time, yet never appears busy. It always has time for relevant things. It is supremely busy creating so much.

Bliss is gained through the practice, state and experience of santosha. It is great bliss and it keeps expanding. Without santosha there is no bliss; without appreciation, without seeing the Is-ness of Is-ness, without the attention to what is here in the Now, you cannot experience its bliss. For the only joy is here and if you don't have the ability to be here in your fullest capacity, then you're not in bliss. When you are here in your fullest capacity, in a state of appreciation and gratefulness, then you are naturally in a bliss state.

कायेन्द्रियसिद्धिरशुद्धिक्षयात् तपसः ॥ ४३ ॥

2:43 Kayendriya siddhirashuddhikshayat tapasah

Through the practice of tapas, we are able to purify the body, clear it of toxins, and so the mind becomes clear and our sense organs become more intuitive. As we continue to practice tapas, we find we become much more perceptive. Our senses become more refined, more finely tuned, and we are able to draw more information in through them. We can then enjoy far more through our senses. The body starts to become stronger through the discipline of tapas, through testing oneself, and the toxins start to be destroyed. When we do a particular kriya over a particular length of time, say for example, three months, and we stay with it, a radical effect starts to happen. That is tapas. If you do something consistently, you gain incredible strength, your mind becomes purified, your senses become clearer, you become stronger. It will naturally happen even if you make a commitment for just two months. Any tapas practice will make you stronger. Taking a cold shower daily or not using your phone first thing in the morning will make you stronger.

Patanjali is saying that through tapas, we start to gain a greater power not just over our body but also over our senses. Our mind clears. With a clear mind we develop strong willpower and willpower is one of the great allies. We need to have that navel power and the way to develop navel power is through tapas. We need it on our journey through space and time. Some people think willpower is against surrender and that surrender and will are separate, but this is not the case. A surrendered will is the hallmark of the yogi. When you have total surrender to what Is, then you have strength and will, together simultaneously.

स्वाध्यायाद् इष्टदेवतासंप्रयोगः ॥ ४४॥

2:44 Svadhyayad ishtadevata sanprayogah

Through the practice of svadhyaya, one gains greater and greater self-awareness, greater and greater self-realization, and one becomes closer and closer to Ishta. Then one is able to experience union as expressed in shape and form. If your knowledge of yourself, your true Self, is increasing, then it is bound to happen. It has to accompany the experience of closer communion with the Divine. A sense of sacredness becomes much more available to you as you practice svadhyaya, as you observe yourself. Then you naturally develop a greater capacity to be in tune with god, with Ishta, the Divine. It will just naturally start to happen.

समाधिसिद्धिरीश्वरप्रणिधानात् ॥ ४५॥

2:45 Samadhi siddhir ishvarapranidhanat

Patanjali says that through the practice of ishvarapranidhanat samadhi becomes much more accessible, through moving in the direction of unity, through ishvarapranidhanat. Of course, through surrender we gain unity. When you surrender your ego, you surrender your doubt, you surrender your complaining, you surrender everything. The value of your surrender is directly proportional to the value of your unity. The unity you experience is directly proportional to the level of surrender you have. And this surrender is the act of the strong not the weak.

Surrender involves one's will. It is not an act of weakness, it is the act of great strength. That is why samadhi is the gift of ishvarapranidhanat. Devotion, deep surrender, gives us access to greater perfection in unity. Love gives love, through love you experience more love, you give more love and so, of course, you experience more love. That's the law. Stupid people are always looking for what they call love, but their love is a trap. They lay careful traps with their love, like catching a cockerel in the forest. In India, when I was a kid, we would go into the forest and find all this thread work tied between the trees. It was a trap to catch the wild birds so when they got their foot caught in the thread, they couldn't fly away. Like the ignorant who use love like a carefully laid out trap, they weave their love to tie you in knots. That is not love, not true love; love is never used to ensnare anyone. The law of the universe is what? The love you give is the love you get, the love you experience. So if you give love, you experience love, ishvarapranidhanat. Surrender is one of the highest expressions of love, you surrender and you experience love. The more you love, then the more you experience love, love that is free and liberating, love that is totally illuminating.

स्थिरसुखम् आसनम् ॥ ४६ ॥

2:46 Sthira sukham asanam

This is the only sutra where Patanjali discusses asana, but he is not merely speaking about the physical posture in which to meditate. He is also talking about embodying the state of consciousness not just on the level of thought. He is saying that the state of yoga, this incredible immense knowledge, has to be physically embodied. It has to be effortlessly present in your own consciousness and if it is effortlessly present, you will find natural bliss arising.

The first asana, the primary asana, is that you embody the teachings in all aspects of your life. That is the fundamental asana, to effortlessly embody the teachings in all the dimensions of your life without a struggle. To be effortlessly devoted and through your devotion, you effortlessly start to embody sthira sukham. As you embody it, you find a deeper and deeper bliss. That is the true asana.

On the level of your mat practice and the asana used in the practice of meditation, the seat should be absolutely comfortable, peace-inducing, enabling stillness. How does one achieve that? One is actually not practicing asana. When you are doing physical practices such as the kriyas, every kriya has a posture to it. There comes a stage in your own practice when you are no longer practicing the asana or the kriya. You are the asana. You are the kriya. That is the goal. As long as you are practicing it, there is a separation between you and the goal, you and the meditation, you and the kriya. Sthira sukham asanam. Patanjali is inviting the practitioner to merge with the practice, inviting you to become the asana, to become the kriya, to become the meditation. Sthira, still. Sukham, peace-inducing, bliss-producing. As you start to embody it, you naturally start experiencing a sense of peace and bliss. Peace and bliss is the natural outcome. As you pour yourself into the practice, with your total attention, you will find a great quality of presence in your practice. There will cease to be anymore separation. Sthira sukham asanam, on the mat and in your life.

प्रयत्नशैथिल्यानन्तसमापत्तिभ्याम्   ॥ ४७ ॥

2:47 Prayatna shaithily ananda samapattibhyam

Patanjali further explains how consistent effort leads to the full absorption of your practice. It is important to realize that when you naturally start to go deeper, you reach a level of integration, a level of synthesis, where the practice is now effortlessly flowing through you and is no longer a struggle. It starts to show up elsewhere too. There is an effortless ease in your life. You will find that you start to accomplish much more in much less time and with much less effort. The things you do, you do in an absolutely present manner with the optimal amount of energy flowing through you. Living your life does not feel like any kind of an effort. When the state of consciousness of an individual is object-dominated, life can feel like hard work. It's quite tragic that we have been the architects of a world we don't want to live in, that so many of us have actually designed lives for ourselves from which we want to take a break, that are burdensome to us and in which we struggle. For some reason, humanity has decided to accept that suffering is a part of life, that one must suffer. But if the practice is continuous, then your capacity to live a life to its full value will increase. You will feel more alive, more alert, yet it will feel effortless, meaning it will cease to be stressful. You will experience an absence of stress.

One only achieves this stress-free existence, mind you, through consistent practice, through self-mastery, taking oneself to the edge, pushing oneself to the limit, challenging oneself, breaking the barrier of one's own perceived limitations within the context of thought. As that consistency becomes a part of one's life, then a new quality of presence starts to arise and with it, a highly creative life of effortless ease. But first, effort is required and continuous practice in all aspects of your life. It's an important point to realize, because some people start with effort, they stay with effort and they die with effort. They did not progress at all. They just kept their practice on a piece of rubber mat, usually about 6 foot by 3. This is not the practice we're interested in. We're approaching yoga as a whole life experience, which includes the meditation practice and the asanas, but we are also taking it beyond the walls of the shala. The yoga studio is only a very recent phenomenon. Through effort, one arrives at a state of expansion, integration and experience and then the effortlessness starts to arrive. It's the end of the struggle. Then you will find that you are more active, but you are not restless. You have a stillness within you which will allow you to be more engaged in what you do. You will have a greater radiance, a greater scope of influence, a greater sense of humility and ability to surrender to life. In the context of the techniques and practice, in your sadhana, now it will be integrated in you. You are the sadhana. You are the asana. You are the pranayama. You are the astanga that Patanjali is referring to here, the astanga, the eight limbs of yoga, meaning the eight aspects of yoga. The state of consciousness that is experiencing yoga emanates these qualities.

ततो द्वन्द्वानभिघातः ॥ ४८ ॥

2:48 Tato dvandvah anabhighatah

Patanjali continues to discuss the natural progression that occurs in evolution. As the practitioner evolves, they are no longer split within their psyche, no longer pulled in opposite directions. They have transcended their resistance and arrived at a new state of consciousness. As the resistance drops away, it is replaced with devotion. Devotion arises, devotion to your practice, a love affair and in that love there is no opposition. So the practitioner begins to experience a greater ease, a sense of flow within their psyche. They will break the pattern of self-sabotage, self-importance and self-obsession, these lower qualities of the mind. "I am the best, I am the worst, I want this, I don't want that, I crave aversion." This constant thunder, this constant wrestling match, is now transcended through consistency in one's practice, experience and state of yoga, through this continued awareness. As you start to experience this state, you are liberated from this split within you and this quality of wholeness starts to show up clearly, in all aspects of your life. Wherever you are, you are wholly there, fully there, in your practice. Not 50%, not 60%, not 80%, because you have transcended that resistance, this half-assing attitude which as we know makes nature scream in agony. You will no longer have this tendency to show up somewhere and not be fully present, not fully committed, with a split psyche and your attention all over the place. In yoga this split cannot stay, it has to synthesize.

तस्मिन् सति श्वासप्रश्वासयोर्गतिविच्छेदः

2:49 Tasmin sati shvasa prashvasayor gativichchhedah pranayamah

In sutras 49 to 53 of Pada 2, Patanjali begins to explore pranayama. The word prana pre-existed his Yoga Sutras, so we can be pretty certain that he would already have had an understanding of pranayama, knowledge which would have come to him through the oral tradition. The yogi already understood, on the level of his being, that this manifested reality, both within and without, is primarily energy, is prana. That there is nothing, no stone, rock or crystal, not a flower or a tree, not an animal or even the very body you currently inhabit, that is not energy, that is not prana. Once we start to refine our intellect and our understanding of the nature of the world, we can then start to tune our relationship with and our understanding of, this energy within.

First, Patanjali discusses pranayama within the context of the breath, but it is very important for us not to limit our understanding, and therefore its possibilities by translating pranayama as breath control. That is not what pranayama means. Prana means energy, yama means tuning. So the word pranayama really means the art, the practice and the state where our understanding is aligned, is tuned, with the natural law, through the practices and techniques which help us to achieve this. The natural law being that the nature of all essential, all manifested, reality is intelligent energy. This is energy, which is conscious, this is intelligent energy. For the fundamental nature of the world, of shape and form, is energetic; it is vibrating. Everything that seems static to us is actually vibrating, energy vibrating, because it is the nature of energy to vibrate. So for energy to vibrate in the context of a chair, where it retains its chair-ness, there definitely has to be an intelligence. When that same energy vibrates as a piece of flat wood, it stays a piece of wood. When it vibrates as a rock, it stays as a rock and when that rock is chiseled and crafted into a piece of sculpture, then it vibrates as a piece of sculpture. It is very clear that this energy is intelligent. It is very ignorant of human beings, even though their own body is an intelligent expression of this very same energy and so is constant proof that intelligence is contained in this energy, to think of this energy as being deprived of any intelligence and actually refer to it as inert, to say for instance, a rock is an inert object. That is what the yogis refer to as prana, often also called shakti, the divine feminine energy.

In the context of the Yoga Sutras, when the word pranayama is used, Patanjali already assumes that those who are reading or listening to the sutras, understand that the nature of reality is energy, that everything you see around you, all manifested expressions are intelligent energy vibrating at different frequencies, in different forms. Including the very body that you call self or me or I. Once we have this foundation of understanding, our whole worldview starts to alter. The doorway to this prana, this energy, is through the breath; and as we enter the practices of pranayama, based on this refined intelligence and corrected intellect, we do so in the yogic tradition.

In these sutras, Patanjali does not really give any particular techniques. He just touches upon the possibility of prana and the importance of pranayama. For without having access to energy within your body, you cannot refine your nervous system. If you are just working on the surface value of the body, just on the physical level of the body, then the body is weak and so the being is weak. It is only when you have access to prana that you really understand the vitality and health which transcend body image. When the yoga is limited just to the value of the body, it really has no value. The potential for prana is infinite, but only as we move into a deeper dimension of yoga does the importance of the pranayama practices naturally become available to us. Working with the breath is just the beginning of pranayama. It is just an entry point to this infinite field of correcting your perception and learning to see the world as energy. Refining your nervous system allows it to have access to more and more energy. Refining your physiology allows the great Kundalini energy to rise and move through you without resisting the free flow of prana so the body does not go into shock. In other words, it allows a controlled awakening to your own infinite potential.

बाह्याभ्यन्तरस्तम्भवृत्तिः   देशकालसंख्याभिः
परिदृष्टो दीर्घसूक्ष्मः ॥ ५० ॥

2:50 Bahya bhyantara stambha vrittih desha kala sankhyabhih paridrishto dirgha sukshmah

बाह्याभ्यन्तरविषयाक्षेपी चतुर्थः ॥ ५१ ॥

2:51 Bahyabhyantara vishayakshepi chaturthah

In sutras 50 and 51, Patanjali discusses cultivating the breath control to access the subtler dimensions of prana. Anyone who has practiced these techniques will know how this incredible experience starts to dawn as you start to gain deeper access to the experience of no mind. As you gain access to no mind, you also gain a greater mastery over the mind. You can only master your mind when you can access the no mind within your own Self. If you don't have access to no mind, there is no way you can master it. When the dominant awareness is only within the mind, it is very difficult to focus, difficult to separate oneself from the barrage of thoughts that constantly seem to be transmitted, the neurons that constantly seem to be firing. It is only when the individual starts to have access to no mind that they can start to master their mind. The pranayama practices are of incredible value to us in accessing the state of no mind. Through the practice and understanding of pranayama and through refining that understanding, when you start to relate to the nature of reality on the level of prana, then the light starts to pierce through and the wheel of ignorance is broken. From the yogi's perspective, yoga can only serve our life when it is understood in its fullest expression. When yoga is only understood in its isolated, conceptual value as a form of physical exercise, which seems to be happening a lot in our world today, then it loses its value. The true value of yoga disappears. For the true value of yoga to remain, it has to be understood, practiced, and experienced at its full value.

ततः क्षीयते प्रकाशावरणम् ॥ ५२ ॥

2:52 Tatah ksiyate parkas avaranam

Patanjali makes it very clear that through the practice of pranayama, we can increase our level of vitality and start to go into no mind. Continued practice will naturally start to give us access to this no mind. Most people locate themselves, their sense of self or ego, their dominant identity, inside their skull, just a few inches behind their eyes and below the top of their head. But through the practice of pranayama, you will start to have access to an intelligence beyond that. Then you can really start moving to the level of chitta, pure consciousness and wisdom. It is then possible, when doing the kriyas which involve prana practices, to gain access to an experience which has a transcendental value, an experience which is incredibly empowering and gives you the possibility to get in touch with your wisdom, your inner light.

धारणासु च योग्यता मनसः ॥ ५३ ॥

2:53 Dharanasu ch yojnata manasah

Through the practices of pranayama, pratyahara and kriya, the mind becomes naturally more fluid, Patanjali says. With this fluid awareness, it becomes capable of greater concentration and so becomes naturally ready for dharana.

स्वस्वविषयासंप्रयोगे चित्तस्य स्वरूपानुकार इवेन्द्रियाणां प्रत्याहारः ॥ ५४ ॥

2:54 Svasvavishaya asanprayoge chittasya svarupanukara ivendriyanan pratyahara

As I have said before, the eight limbs of yoga: yama, niyama, asana, pranayama, pratyahara, dharana, dhyana and samadhi, are not steps to yoga. They are different aspects of the body of yoga, the state of yoga, the practice of yoga and the experience of yoga. Pratyahara is the withdrawing of the senses. Pratya meaning to move the senses in the opposite direction of their natural tendency, since their natural tendency is to flow outward, because the dominant meaning of life is still residing only in the mind, at the brain level. When this tendency is opposed, it changes the movement and directs the senses inward. Pratyahara untangles the awareness from the senses and frees it from the need to derive a meaning, so you are no longer bound by them. In the beginning, you may experience pratyahara as a singular awareness of withdrawing the senses. But the state of dual awareness will occur as you become the witness of that withdrawal inward, the experiencer becomes the experience.

Closing our eyes and covering our head with a shawl to insulate ourselves are very helpful techniques when we are sitting down to meditate, so we can really be in our meditation practice and turn our senses inward. In the greater practice of pratyahara, the state of pratyahara and the experience of pratyahara, as you turn the attention inward, turning it toward the source, you will start to experience the natural withdrawal of the senses. Now, you will no longer be so obsessed with the manifest world and the values you have given it. It can no longer hijack your awareness, because your awareness is no longer moving outward. Although some of your thoughts are coming from your subconscious, many of them are actually outside you. Even though you are experiencing them inside your brain, they are really just being caught by your mind.

As we turn our awareness inside, to the source value of Self, the ultimate subject, it then becomes the object. Consciousness starts to become aware of its own Self. The consciousness starts to turn and look at itself, that is why we call it Self-realization. In your mundane life, when your attention is moving out, the senses are also moving in the outward direction. When you start to practice pratyahara, you are establishing dual attention. You're walking, you're talking, you're driving, you're eating, you're at the office. Wherever you are, there is also part of your awareness moving inward, in the direction of Self. You witness it and you are aware of the experiencer experiencing it. There is Self and there is non-self. Before one can reach the state of Self-realization, one has to go through this state where one is firmly established in the practice, awareness and experience of Self and non-self. The subject value then starts to dominate space in the field of consciousness, which is now aware of its own Self, witnessing its own Self. That is also called mindfulness, a very popular word today.

As you become more and more established in the state of pratyahara, what starts to happen is that you find an inner stillness. Even though there is movement occurring, your body is moving and talking and walking and so on, you will witness this sense of silent presence. It's what Rumi calls the silent one, it who has never spoken out loud. It only speaks when you are silent and it is silent when you speak, for you can only hear it in your great depth of silence; this silent one who speaks very softly becomes stronger and stronger within you. Cultivating our awareness of this silent one within, of turning our attention inward through the techniques of pranayama, meditation and kriya, refines our nervous system. As we refine our nervous system, we start to create the capacity for our attention to flow in both directions. It can keep flowing in the direction of the mundane reality, the manifest world, but it can also flow in the direction of the subject. So when you are doing your deeper sadhana, your meditation practice, then it starts to flow at its fullest value toward the internal reality, toward the source. Then you are transcending feelings, thoughts, emotions, transcending the subconscious mind, and ultimately going to the field of bliss consciousness. Sat chit ananda, the state of bliss. That is pratyahara.

ततः परमा वश्यतेन्द्रियाणाम् ॥ ५५ ॥

2:55 Tath parama vasyatendriyanam

Through pratyahara, there is mastery of the senses. What Patanjali means here is mastery over the mind, because it is through the senses that the lower mind receives all its impressions. The senses are our windows to the world. There are three distinct kinds of optical cells within the optical nerve. So when we see the light, we are capable of seeing thousands of different colors within it. Depending on what wavelength we use, we are able to see thousands of different shades of color. But it's a two-way process. We use our senses to absorb the world, but also our mind projects on to this. Like the man who thinks he is seeing a snake that is actually a rope. The conditioned mind can also project, for example, that this person doesn't like me. Now when one looks at that person, one always sees that. Their body language looks negative, their attitude feels negative, but that person is actually not doing anything negative. It is all in one's mind. It's all projection.

So through pratyahara, as we draw the senses toward the source, we naturally start to gain mastery over them. The senses are not the perception of reality. They are not affected by the lower mind anymore. Through pratyahara, you will gain a cosmic mind and cosmic senses with a greater value, not the dull senses of a dull mind. A heightened awareness has heightened senses. By taking the senses in the direction of the Absolute, keeping them in the Absolute, then exposing them to the relative reality, the senses have the capacity to perceive the Absolute while enjoying the relative values within the field of the Absolute. One then doesn't lose the perception of the Absolute while enjoying the fruits on the surface: riding a motorcycle, enjoying an adventure, sharing a meal, enjoying all that is available on the surface value. But now, at no time does one lose the perception of the Absolute. The surface is not able to dominate the field of your awareness completely. You are able to maintain the awareness of the field while enjoying the movements arising in the field of god. That is the gift that pratyahara starts to give you. You can enjoy through your senses, but your awareness is maintained at the cosmic level. Then the sensory experience starts to take on the cosmic value.

All sensory experience is actually designed to do that. That is why there is such ecstasy in sensory experience. If such experiences were so terrible for our species, we would not have evolved to be able to enjoy such a range of diverse ecstasy through our senses. Our species has evolved to be unlike an amoeba, that is just there, reproducing all by itself. Very boring. Who wants to be an amoeba? Nobody wants to be an amoeba. When we look at human beings, we can see how we have evolved. There is a corresponding increase in our capacity to experience bliss in the relative field of reality. That is evolution. An ant is only interested in food. If you say, "Hey ant, let's go and enjoy Mozart," it's not going to be interested. But through our senses, we can appreciate a woman on a stage wearing a beautiful, elegant dress, playing Mozart. This is a step up from the ant just chasing the sugar.

The universe cannot be manifesting just for the purpose of surface value pleasures. So naturally, all our sensory experience has the capacity to give us a view into the cosmos, because it is only the cosmos that is experiencing itself. The supreme Self is experiencing the supreme Self back. Through pratyahara, we direct the senses toward the supreme Self in its absolute state. Then when the senses are exposed to the relative field of reality, they will still maintain the awareness. The individual is then able to maintain the awareness of the cosmic Being and to enjoy the relative field to its fullest extent, as it should be enjoyed. It is there to be enjoyed. Nobody lays on their deathbed saying, "Wow, I'm so happy I did not eat that chocolate cake," or, "I'm so grateful I skipped my lunch, I'm so happy I did not dance, so grateful I did not enjoy myself." You can see the people who have lived a full life. You can find that at their core is a great fragrance. They are still alive even in the moment of their death. Then there are people who have not lived their life at all and they die long before their physical death.

As we achieve a greater and greater mastery over our senses, meaning that they are not able to confuse us and the lower mind is not able to blur our perception, but is more and more refined and rises up to its true potential, our mind then becomes our ally. Our senses become our ally.

Got it or not?

Glossary of Sanskrit Words

A

Ahimsa	transcendence of violence
Ananda	bliss
Asamprajnata	highest stage of samadhi
Asana	seat, physical posture
Asmita	I am-ness
Atman	soul
Avidya	incorrect knowledge, ignorance

B

Brahmanas	a collection of ancient Indian texts

C

Chitta	pure consciousness

D

Dharana	concentration of thought, to focus our awareness on an internal event
Dharma	living a purposeful and evolutionary life
Dhyana	meditation

G

Guru	spiritual teacher

H

Himsa	violence

J

Japa	meditative repetition of a mantra or divine name
Jiva	any entity imbued with a life force

K

Karma	actions that lead to bondage and suffering
Kundalini	infinite potential of Being, coiled serpent at the base of the spine

M

Mumukshutva	a great desire for liberation

N

Nirvichara	lower state of samadhi
Nirvikalpa	free from doubt, unwavering

P

Prajna	continued awareness
Prakrti	unmanifested cosmic energy
Prana	energy
Pratyahara	withdrawal of the senses
Punya	good, pure, meritorious

R

Rajas	movement, activated

S

Sadhaka	spiritual aspirant
Sadhana	your practice of mindful living and sacred daily rituals
Samadhi	unity consciousness
Santosha	contentment, grace
Sanveganam	those who are quick to practice, are moving toward non-victim identity
Samskara	mental impressions that affect our perception, conditioning which is limiting
Satori	awakening
Sattva	pure
Satya	truth
Siddhi	seemingly supernatural ability
Shakti	divine feminine energy

T

Tamas	unmotivated, lethargic
Tamasic	dissatisfied, materialistic

V

Vichara	clear perception, clear observation
Vidya	knowledge
Vitarka	correct reasoning
Vairagyam	detachment
Vritti	thought or thought pattern that causes a disturbance in consciousness

Made in the USA
Las Vegas, NV
29 October 2021